MW00761086

Shattered Lives

Shattered Lives

The Path To Recovery

Robert Cole

CHAPLAINCY DEPT.

Rainbow's End Company
354 Golden Grove Road
Baden, PA 15005

http://adpages.com/rbebooks

©1998 by Robert F. Cole

Published by Rainbow's End Company
354 Golden Grove Road
Baden, PA 15005

Printed in the United States of America

All rights reserved. No part of this publication may be re-produced, stored in a retrieval system, or transmitted in any form by any means—electronic, mechanical, photocopy, re-cording, or any other—without the prior written permission of the publisher. The only exception is brief quotations in printed reviews.

Cover Design: Susan Vincent

Publisher's Cataloging-in-Publication
(Provided by Quality Books, Inc.)

Cole, Robert Fount.
     Shattered lives : the path to recovery / by Robert F. Cole. -- 1st ed.
     p. cm.
     Preassigned LCCN: 97-7661
     ISBN: 1-880451-27-1

     1. Grief--Religious aspects--Christianity. 2. Suicide. 3. Cole, Robert Fount.   I. Title.

BV4905.2.C65 1998   248.8'66
                           QBI97-41589

To my dear wife, Elsie,
truly, my better half,
who has shared my joys and sorrows
during our
fifty-six years of marriage

CHAPLAINCY DEPT.

Contents

Preface

On July 3, 1941, my wife Elsie and I were married in Coeur d'Alene, Idaho. God has been good to us, blessing us with five sons and eight grandchildren.

I grew up at Moses Lake, Washington, while Elsie was reared at Coeur d'Alene. My parents had an ideal marriage and provided a happy childhood for my sister, my brother and me. Elsie, too, although her father died while she was a teenager, had the advantage of having loving parents throughout her childhood.

Shortly after the birth of our first son, I was called by Uncle Sam to serve in the armed forces during World War II. In 1946, more than a year after the conclusion of the war, I was discharged and returned home where, using the educational benefits of the G.I. Bill of Rights, I attended and graduated from Whitworth College with a B.A. Degree. Later, I received a Master of Education Degree from Central Washington State University and my administrative credentials from the University of Washington.

Elsie chose not to pursue a post-high school education. Instead, she chose to follow the most honorable profession a woman can have—that of mother and homemaker. And what a remarkable homemaker she has been during our more than

56 years of marriage.

My career in education covered a span of 31 years, with the majority of the years served in high school administration. As I pursued and climbed the ladder of success, we lived in the states of Oregon, California and Washington. In 1974 we moved to Pasco, Washington where I served as a high school administrator.

Our home in Pasco was a charming structure, comfortable and spacious with two full floors aboveground comprising of 13 rooms, including an apartment on the lower floor occupied by our youngest son, John. A covered deck, constructed over the attached garage, provided a panoramic view of our mini-farm, numerous fruit trees, and large garden area. We enjoyed our home with its many amenities and pleasures of country living.

After my retirement in 1982, we remained in Pasco until 1988 when we moved to McMinnville, Oregon, where we are currently living. Little did my dear wife and I realize the tragedies that would befall us during a six-year-period in the decade of the eighties.

INTRODUCTION

In two years I would be eligible to retire from public school administration. My wife, Elsie, and I were looking forward to retirement, anticipating the many activities available to us as seniors. Most of all, we were delighted that we would be able to spend more time with our five sons and their families.

But the pleasant plans we made for our lives were not to be. The decade of the eighties proved to be a period of disaster when, in July of 1980, our second son, David, was killed in a dreadful motorcycle accident. We followed the process of grief, nearly reaching recovery when, in September of 1983, our fourth son, Donald, died a horrible death in the crash of his automobile. First David and now Donald! *How*, we wondered, *could we possibly endure the loss of two of our sons?*

Somehow, by the grace of God, we were able to climb from the depths of despair and, once more, nearly reach a point of acceptance. Then in February of 1986 the unthinkable happened—tragedy struck again—our youngest son, John, committed suicide. Our lives were devastated as, for the third time, we were plunged to the depths of despair. We thought that there was no way we could possibly live through three such tragic deaths; however, God embraced us with His love and carried us through our darkest valley.

Our sons were raised in a Christian home; but, were they in the presence of the Master? Through meditation, I sought an answer from God. His love came flooding through the window of my heart filling me with unspeakable joy. The Holy Spirit spoke to me, revealing His presence in a way I had never before experienced. My entire being was shaken as I stood in awe. Completely oblivious to all around me, I was guided by holy angels. Never before, nor since, have I experienced such a feeling of joy and tranquility like the one that filled me at that moment. Truly, I had entered into the presence of God and was given a glimpse of Heaven. There, in my heavenly home, in the beauty of His presence, I saw the full glory of His Kingdom and received my answer. Peace filled me to overflowing as God confirmed the presence of David, Donald, and John in the Kingdom of Heaven. Tears of joy coursed down my cheeks as I shouted praises of thanksgiving!

We can grow through adversity, however, to do so, it is essential that we deal with our loss and complete the grief process. No two people experience or express their grief in the same way, nor can one person bear the grief of another. In preparation for our own death, or the death of a loved one, we all should further our understanding of the death and dying process. The love of Christ in the heart of the believer will greatly reduce the trauma of death.

I have written this book, through the guidance of the Holy Spirit, to aid others through the grief process; to comfort the broken-hearted; to help others realize the pitfalls of danger that exist in dealing with grief; to give direction and purpose to life; to better understand suicide; to aid suicide survivors; to stimulate spiritual growth; and, as a guide to prepare us for our heavenly home.

It is my fervent prayer that the greatest gift of all—God's love—will, through the window of the heart, shine upon every person who reads these words.

CHAPTER ONE

Please God Don't Let Him Die!

Elsie called from the sewing room, "Honey, will you please answer the phone." Reaching for the phone in our bedroom, I said aloud, "I wonder who that can be."

"Bob, this is Jim," followed my greeting. My heart leaped to my throat. It was our son David's friend, his biking buddy. After a short pause, he continued, "David's been in an accident. His motorcycle . . ."

"Oh no!" I cried, "was he badly injured?"

Jim hesitated, "Yes, Bob, he was. His left leg was severed just below the knee. He has other injuries, too, but I don't know how bad they are. The doctor told me that his condition is critical. He . . . he was brought by ambulance to the Valley General Hospital just off Pines Road in Spokane Valley. You had better come right away!"

Struggling to comprehend what he was telling me, I said, "We'll . . . we'll leave immediately. It's about a three hour drive, so expect us about 9:30. Tell David we're on our way!"

"I will," he replied. "And I'll be here waiting for you."

Elsie, who had just entered the room, saw the look of anguish and shock on my face and immediately knew something was wrong. "What is it, Honey?" she anxiously asked.

"David has been seriously hurt in a motorcycle accident! He's lost a leg and has other injuries. He's in Valley General Hospital!"

At first, shocked beyond belief by my words, Elsie stood speechless and motionless, then she cried out in agony, "Oh, David, David!"

We both prayed silently as we hurriedly prepared to leave. While Elsie gathered a few articles of clothing, I quickly jotted a note to our youngest son, John, who was visiting friends. As we backed our little truck out of the garage, I looked over at Elsie, "Let's stop by the church and ask for prayers for David!" Unable to speak, she nodded in agreement, tears streaming down her cheeks.

Parking near the front entrance to the sanctuary, I ran inside. Pastor Strong, standing at the pulpit, was about to open the Sunday evening service. Quickly, I told him what I knew about the accident and requested prayer for David. As I turned to leave, I heard him lift his voice to Heaven in David's behalf.

My thoughts were entirely on David as I left the church parking lot and turned onto the freeway that would take us to Spokane. It was so hard to believe! Elsie and I had just returned home from Spokane a few hours earlier after spending a delightful weekend with David and our two little granddaughters, Katie, six, and Kami, four. But we were apprehensive about his recently acquired motorcycle, and had told him so.

A handsome, virle man of 35, David was 6' 2" with a strapping physique. His ingratiating smile, quick wit and sparkling sense of humor commanded attention in any setting, providing him with an abundance of friends. I couldn't imagine David without his left leg. He was a star athlete in high school, receiving an athletic scholarship to enter the football program at Eastern Washington State University where he continued to

14

play until he was sidelined by a knee injury. He had nearly completed his senior year, but dropped out of college to work full time. This allowed Susan, his wife, to complete college and obtain her teaching degree and certificate. After spending several years managing fund-raising programs for charitable institutions, David eventually took a position as manager of a non-profit bingo establishment. Unfortunately, things didn't work out in their marriage and, after their divorce, Susan was given custody of Katie and Kami. The children, who were the apple of David's eye, spent long carefree weekends with him.

Driving through the evening, I was conscious that Elsie was suffering in silence as only a mother can when her child has been grievously injured. I thought about my lifeline to God—surely the Almighty wouldn't allow David to die! I was worried, but confident that, with God's help, he would survive.

Dusk was turning to darkness when we entered the parking lot of Valley General Hospital. Jim and his wife, Lisa, were waiting for us by the front entrance. Quickly I selected a space, turned off the ignition and lights and, taking Elsie by the hand, went to meet them. Seeing a look of anguish on his face and fearful of what his answer might be, I called out, "Jim, how's David?"

"Bob," he said softly, "David didn't make it! He's dead!"

"Oh no, Jim! Oh no! It can't be!" I cried, gathering Elsie in my arms. The shock of his words was so great I felt as though I had been struck a powerful blow. My knees began to buckle as Elsie went limp in my arms. Jim and Lisa came to stand beside us and offer support. I recall how suddenly angry I became. "God," I cried out through my tears, "why didn't You answer our prayers? Why couldn't You let him live?"

Entering the hospital waiting room we saw Janice Harding, David's girlfriend, and her parents. Seeing us, she quickly came to embrace us.

"Janice," I said, "I just can't believe it! David gone? It

15

doesn't seem possible!"

Janice, sobbing, shook her head in reply.

I barely remember leaving the hospital and driving to David's house. Janice followed us there in her car and stayed with us for a while. Later, we learned that David and Jim had left on their motorcycles at about 2:00 p.m. for a scenic ride along beautiful Coeur d'Alene Lake in Idaho and back through the Spokane Valley of Washington. They were on their way home after a pleasant trip.

Jim was about a mile or so ahead of David and didn't personally witness the accident. Later, however, when he re-constructed the accident, he came to the conclusion that David's motorcycle, for whatever reason, had swerved going around a curve on the outskirts of Rockwell, went over an embankment and crashed into a telephone pole.

Was he going too fast? Did he lose control? Nobody knows! There were no witnesses. If his bike had gone just two feet to the left or right of the pole and into the open field, most likely he would have sustained only minor injuries. Instead, he lay bleeding and unconscious for several minutes before he was discovered by a passerby. A few minutes later an ambulance, returning to Idaho from Spokane, also came upon the accident scene. Unfortunately, they weren't adequately equipped to properly treat David's severe injuries. The para-medics did, however, work feverishly to save his life as they rushed him to the hospital.

Jim, wondering why David hadn't caught up with him, turned his bike around and backtracked through Rockwell Washington where he was horrified to find his friend receiv-ing emergency treatment. He knew from the amount of blood loss from the severed leg and the blood he saw coming from David's mouth, that it was serious and that he might not make it.

It was not long after we arrived at David's house that the phone rang. It was John. He had found my hurriedly written

16

note. As if from a distance, I heard my voice telling him that his brother had not survived the accident. I was startled. It was as though another person, a man who faltered and was torn with grief, were speaking. John was stunned and speechless. Finally, in a quaking voice, he said, "Dad, I'm on my way."

We were now faced with the difficult task of calling our other sons. Mike, our middle son, who lived in Corvallis, Oregon, received the news with difficulty, stunned by shock and disbelief, as did Donald, our fourth son, and Bill, our eldest.

When John arrived, he was so overcome with emotion that his mother and I held him in our arms for almost an hour.

I held my dear wife as we lay in bed. We were awake the whole night through, our tears intermingling as they fell softly to the pillow.

Anger arose within me—I was bitterly angry with God for allowing our son to be taken from us. When I later read the Elizabeth Kubler-Ross book about death and dying, these feelings of anger were sustained. She wrote, "When the first stage of denial cannot be maintained any longer, it is replaced by feelings of anger, rage, envy and resentment. The logical question becomes; 'Why me?' "

Making my anger even more intense were my thoughts about the splendid father-son relationship that David and I had. We were very close, regularly confiding in and seeking one another's advice. We enjoyed watching sports together on television and going to games, especially traveling to the Kingdome in Seattle to watch the Seahawks play. "Oh God, how I love that boy!" I cried aloud. "Why God? Why did You take him from me?"

When Jim and Lisa told us that David was dead, not only did my world of hope for David come crashing down but, belatedly, I began to question my unchallenged faith in God. Tragedies like this were not supposed to happen to honest deserving people who had spent their lives following the "Good Book" and loving God. Yes, loving Him as the Supreme Ruler of the universe, but also loving Him as the One who provides a destination for us when our life on earth is over.

After reading Rabbi Harold Kushner's book, *When Bad Things Happen To Good People*, my feelings of anger were somewhat abated. He was speaking to Elsie and me when he wrote:

> Like most people, my wife and I had grown up with an image of God as an all-wise, all-powerful parent figure who would treat us as our earthly parents did, or even better. If we were obedient and deserving, He would reward us. If we got out of line, He would discipline us, reluctantly, but firmly. He would protect us from being hurt or hurting ourselves, and would see to it that we got what we deserved from life.
>
> Like most people, I was aware of the human tragedies that darkened the landscape—the young people who die in car crashes, the cheerful, loving people wasted by crippling diseases, the neighbors and relatives, whose retarded and mentally ill children, people spoke of in hushed tones. But that awareness never drove me to wonder about God's justice, or to question His fairness. I assumed that He knew more about the world than I.

Copyright © 1981 by Harold S. Kushner.
Copyright © 1989 by Harold S. Kushner. Reprinted by permission of Schocken Books, distributed by Pantheon Books, a division of Random House, Inc.

"Honey, do you think David was prepared to meet God?" Elsie asked.

"Yes, Darling, I think he was. He was raised in a Christian home and faithfully attended Sunday School and church. But even more importantly, he often expressed his faith and belief in Jesus as his Savior. Yes, I firmly believe that he was prepared and is, right at this moment, in Heaven rejoicing with his Lord and the loved ones who have gone before."

The following day, Michael and John assisted us in notifying friends and relatives. Throughout the day, especially after the news of the accident was reported in the newspaper, we received many calls and visits from people wishing to express their condolences. The printed words gave the facts with a cold, detached reality:

Motorcycle Hits Pole,
Kills Rider Near Rockford

A 35 year old Spokane man died Sunday of injuries he received in a motorcycle accident half a mile south of Rockford, Washington.

David R. Cole, N2526 Long Road, died at Valley General Hospital at 7:25 p.m. because of a massive blood loss, the Washington State Patrol reported.

He was riding northwest on Hoxie Road when he rounded a curve to the right, went off the road to the left, entered a ditch and struck a pole, Trooper David Booth said.

Cole was wearing a helmet at the time of the smashup, Booth said.

The motorcycle accident occurred about 6:00 p.m.

Donald arrived late in the afternoon and, as a family, we spent the entire evening in seclusion. It was a time for us to grieve together, discuss David's untimely death, vent our feelings, express our love for David and one another, and pray. Bill, on the advice of his doctor, did not come.

The following day, Elsie and I drove to the mortuary to make funeral arrangements. Our sons offered to go with us; however, we declined. Even though we knew it would be painful, we felt that we alone should be involved in making the arrangements. At the mortuary we had the opportunity to view David's body, to touch and kiss him, and to face the reality of his death. Holding hands, we tuned in to Heaven and committed our son to God.

The funeral service was held on Thursday. The church was filled to capacity with family and friends. Pastor Willis E. Shane was the officiate with Pastor Donald Strong assisting. My brother-in-law, Pastor Shane, along with my sister Shirley, were pillars of strength during the ordeal.

After taking care of David's affairs, we returned to our home where our pastors, close friends from the church, neighbors, coworkers, and others came to comfort us. Although appreciated, all the support in the world couldn't remove the hurt that continued to tear at our hearts.

What, I thought, *have I done or failed to do that might have angered God and brought His wrath upon us. Is God, through David's death, punishing me? I should have died, not him. He was so young and had so much to live for. At 60, I've lived a good life and probably don't have too many more years.*

One evening, perhaps six weeks after David's death, Elsie and I found John sitting in the back yard by himself, wrestling with the same question. "Why?" he asked. "Why did Dave have to die and leave his children? Why didn't God take me instead?" When he shared these thoughts with us, we realized how important it was to allow him, and our other children, to openly express their grief. We dealt with them collectively and individually, and they counseled with one another. We spent quality time with Katie and Kani discussing their father's life, death, and the joy that will be theirs when they join him in Paradise.

All through this period of severe hurting, I was aware of the deep valley that my wife was going through. *I knew because I was experiencing the same journey.* My love for her forced me to sustain and uphold her even in my own despair. In her love she was experiencing the same feelings toward me for all the same reasons.

When I returned to work, my busy schedule, along with a

program of physical fitness, proved helpful. Elsie became busily engaged in her house and yard work. We both resumed our church activities and made our peace with David's death, accepting it as God's will, not understanding the loss, but neither challenging God's authority. Neither of us could possibly imagine another blow befalling us.

One evening, perhaps six weeks after David's death, Elsie and I walked out onto the deck of our house to watch the sunset. As the beautiful colors faded, God's rich blessing filled my soul. I knew that David had joined our Savior beyond the sunset. With that thought in my mind, and with a smile on my face, I began singing the song *Beyond the Sunset*. This was the same song that had been sung at David's funeral. Elsie joined me in the singing as I held her closely.

CHAPTER TWO

A Call In The Night

The day Don caught his four pound trout, I certainly had no premonition of another disaster. From the bow of the boat, Donald shouted, "Fish on! Oh boy! Did you see him jump, Pop? Looks to be at least 20 inches long!" He was nearly bursting with excitement. "I'll bet it's a four pounder, maybe five!"

Throwing the motor into neutral, I quickly brought in my line and watched as Don carefully fought the fish. As soon as he brought it in close enough, I reached for the fish net and, lowering it under the fish, scooped it from the water. "It's at least four pounds, Don. Do you want me to throw it back?" I teased, releasing the fish from the net and watching it flop about on the bottom of the boat.

"If you do, you'll follow the fish!" he retorted, proudly picking up the fish to check it out.

Brandy, Don's seven year old daughter pleaded, "Grandpa, let me fish, too. Please, Grandpa!" Courtney, her four year old sister who we lovingly called "Coco" was content just to watch.

"Okay, Bran, you can use Grandpa's pole," I replied.

Restarting the boat motor and shifting into forward, both Don and I began letting out our lines. When I had released about 200 feet of line, I hit the reel brake and handed the rod to Brandy.

I had just leaned back in the boat to relax when Brandy suddenly screamed, "Grandpa! Grandpa! I caught a fish!" Sure enough, the tip of her pole was rapidly bobbing up and down. I slipped the motor out of gear.

"Let Grandpa show you how to bring it in," I said, as I took hold of her hand and helped her turn the reel handle with her tiny fingers. "Keep your pole up and don't stop reeling. That's it, keep that fish on!" I think I was more excited than Brandy.

I reached for the net. "That's it, honey! Keep the pole tip up! Ah, I got it!" I exclaimed, carefully lifting her trophy out of the water. It was a nice fish—almost two pounds!

We were fishing on beautiful Lake Kookanusa, a reservoir behind Libby Dam in northwest Montana. The lake extends far into Canada and provides many fine fresh-water salmon for sportsmen fishing its waters. The mountains rising from two to three thousand feet above the lake appear to reach for the blue Montana skies.

We agreed that with Brandy's catch we would call it a day and return to the boat landing near our camp.

Don and Paula married shortly after we moved to Pasco in 1974 and decided to stay in Fresno where he worked for the City Parks and Recreation Department. Now, following David's death, they decided to move to Pasco to be near us. No doubt their decision to move was influenced somewhat by Elsie and me who hoped that having them near would somehow help ease the loss of David.

Prior to moving from Fresno, Don obtained employment with a meat processing company in Pasco. It wasn't exactly the kind of job he wanted, but he decided to take it temporarily until something more suitable came along. He also found a comfortable little duplex for his family. They moved in the summer while school was out so that Brandy could enter her new school at the beginning of the 1980-1981 school year.

Don's confidence that he would find a better job paid off. He was exuberant when a contractor at the Hanford Nuclear Reservation hired him for a permanent position at a high rate of pay.

A soft spoken, congenial young man of 26, with big brown eyes and naturally curly brown hair, Don was considered a real "hunk" by the young females in and around our community. He took exceptional care of his body, working out daily and carefully watching his diet and weight. He was always meticulous in dress and appearance. All through junior and senior high school he was active in sports until a serious knee injury, that required surgery, sidelined him from the two sports he enjoyed most—football and basketball.

Don, a talented musician, was especially adept at playing the guitar. He would sit on the floor and play for hours at a time. Brandy and Coco loved to have their daddy play for them at bedtime. The girls responded well to his soft, lilting voice. He rarely found it necessary to raise his voice in discipline—usually just a word was sufficient.

His warm personality enabled him to relate well to others in the workplace, at social gatherings, and in dealing with people in general. Elsie and I looked upon him with great pride; therefore, it came as a great surprise when, in the fall of 1981, his marriage with Paula became strained and began to erode. They had been so devoted to each other and to their daughters that separation and divorce hardly seemed possible.

"Honey, I just can't believe that they're breaking up," I said to Elsie. "Don is progressing so well with his work and—with their new place and all—you'd think that they'd be riding on top of the world."

"I know Hon, it's hard to understand," she replied. Then, after a short pause, added, "Or accept."

Paula and the girls returned to Fresno prior to Christmas and the divorce became final the following spring. Their hopes and dreams for their lives together were shattered.

When a farmer north of Pasco decided to divide his farm into five acre tracts, I agreed to make the down payment for Don and John so that they would have their first real property. By the summer of 1981, the boys had a fine field of alfalfa growing, a horse grazing in their pasture, and a vegetable garden. I even helped them plant fruit trees for a family orchard. In a short time, the kids did wonders with the landscaping and even made plans to build an addition onto the mobile home they shared.

Even though John was three years younger than Don, they were close companions. John was helpful and an uplifting influence to Don during the difficult times following his divorce.

One evening, in early September of 1982, John ascended the stairs that led up into our living room from the recreation room below. "Hi, Mom. Hi, Pop."

"Hi, Son. How are things going? What have you been up to lately beside working?"

"Nothing in particular Pop." Then, with hesitation, he added, "But I am concerned about Don. He's been shirking his responsibility lately, even calling off from work a lot. That's not like him!"

"I've noticed it too," Elsie said. "He's been a bit down lately. Hopefully, he will visit us soon so we can talk with him."

On this indecisive note, we left the subject of Don. Elsie did, however, call him that evening and invite him over for Sunday dinner the next day.

When he arrived, he greeted us with a cheerful, "Hi Mom and Dad." His girlfriend Marcia was with him. "Hope you don't mind me bringing Marcia along."

"Of course we don't son. How are you, Marcia?" Elsie

inquired.

She smiled. "I'm just fine."

"Hi kids," I added as I folded my newspaper and placed it on the coffee table, turning my attention to Don. "How are things going, Son?"

"Not so good, Pop—I lost my job! But it's okay though because I had planned on quitting anyway—been in a quandary for some time. Actually, it will be kind of a relief to get away from Hanford. I'm certain that the change will improve my health both mentally and emotionally. I am going to take a job at St. Michelle, a vineyard and winery down by Patterson."

I was familiar with St. Michelle's. Their vineyards were young but producing quite well and their winery was still under construction. Disappointed with Don's decision, I made my feelings known to him.

"The job won't be forever," he said, somewhat defensively. "As I mentioned before, Pop, I'm thinking of going to Seattle and try my luck at modeling men's clothing."

His idea to model men's fashions came as no surprise to us. He possessed clean, handsome looks, and a sort of subdued attractiveness girls referred to as "sexy."

Don started at the winery within a few days and, shortly thereafter, John was employed there as well. In late May, the winery held an open house for the employees and their families. The boys invited Elsie and me to join them and their girlfriends at the party. We had a good time together. Shortly afterwards, Don and Marcia broke up and Marcia moved back to Seattle.

About the same time Don and John decided to move out of their trailer on the farm. They had lived there for the winter, but Don didn't want to remain and John, by himself, could not afford the payments. They decided to return home and share John's old downstairs apartment. I bailed them out financially by buying out their equities in the mini-farm and arranging to lease it.

One evening in June we were sitting around the living room listening to Don play his guitar. Suddenly he stopped playing, looked at us, and said, "Mom . . . Pop . . . I've decided to move back to California. I've applied for a position with the Fish and Game Department. I'll have to take the civil service exam, but, after all, I do have three years experience in the Department."

I offered him encouragement. "With your experience, training and knowledge, you should have no difficulty passing the exam. "

He smiled appreciatively. "They have some excellent opportunities for photographers in the Department; I'd like to be seriously considered for such a position."

Elsie, the proud mother, asked, "Won't the awards you won in photo exhibits, and your pictures that appeared in photographic journals be a plus?"

"It should certainly help," he replied. Then, choosing his words carefully, he continued. "There's more. I'm . . . I'm hoping that Paula and I can reconcile our differences and get back together. I sure miss her and the girls!"

Outwardly, Elsie and I quietly expressed our satisfaction with his plans to revive his marriage. Inwardly, we were jubilant. The balance of that evening was memorable. Don had written a song about his two girls that he shared with us. He entitled his song *Sisters*. As he sang, strumming his guitar, our hearts were stirred by the beauty of the words. It was so moving.

<u>SISTERS</u>

There are two girls, who are in my mind
They are, my daughters, with their eyes so bright
And I love them both so much.

Even though, they are, both so far away

27

My heart, is with them, so much it's hard to say
Soon I hope I'll be with those two.
Brandy, Courtney, two names mean love to me
Please wait, don't grow, 'till you are with me
I want so much to be with you two.

Green eyes, brown eyes, I see them every day
I hope, and I pray, that soon I'll hear them say,
"Daddy, we want so much to be with you."

By August, Don had completed all the necessary arrangements to take the California State Civil Service Examination and made plans to return to Fresno by the middle of September.

On the morning of September 12, 1983, I arose from the breakfast table and said, "I told the fellow that leases the farm that I'd go out this morning and take care of the irrigation system."

"Wait a minute, Pop, I'll get my jacket and go with you," Don called out as he headed for the downstairs apartment.

We had a terrific day together and talked endlessly about his plans and aspirations upon his return to California. I was pleased to see his enthusiasm.

As we were driving home, Don said, "Pop, if you don't mind, I think I'll ride over to Spokane with you and Mom when you go to see Bill and Pam. I won't have another opportunity to see them before I leave."

"Good idea, son. We'll be pleased to have you along and I'm sure Bill and Pam will be glad to see you. There is one place you can't go though."

"Where's that, Pop?"

"With your Mom and me to the annual seniors' church picnic. We're leaving early tomorrow morning for their campground north of Spokane. And," I said with a chuckle, "You're not old enough yet to qualify as a senior."

We arrived home late in the afternoon to the pleasant smell of dinner being prepared by Elsie. I was famished and could hardly wait. In just a matter of minutes, she called the boys to dinner over the intercom. John quickly responded and took his place at the table, while Don, who was trying to lose a few pounds, indicated that he was going to forego dinner and work out instead.

About a half hour later he came to the top of the stairs and said, "That was a fantastic workout. I really feel good."

At the time I was sitting in my favorite chair watching the evening news. I can clearly recall his muscular shoulders, shining with perspiration; his brown wavy hair, and big brown eyes. My heart went out to him as I silently prayed that God would continue to guide his pathway in life. We chatted for a few minutes.

Elsie, always the concerned mother, admonished him, "Don, I still think you should eat something."

"No, Mom, you're not going to talk me into it this time. I have to trim down a bit. Now, if you folks will excuse me, I'm going to go take a shower."

It wasn't until 9:30 that evening that we missed Don. When John asked us where he had gone, I realized we hadn't seen Don since he'd gone to take a shower.

"I don't know, I assumed he was downstairs."

John, with obvious concern, said, "His station wagon is gone and he knows he shouldn't be driving without a license. He never should have let his California license expire."

I agreed, knowing that he'd decided to wait until he returned to California to renew it. "Maybe he's just gone over to visit with his friends at the new development on the hill."

"Yes," Elsie said, "That's probably where he is."

Though our words were calming to John, I personally felt some anxiety.

Despite my feelings, I said to Elsie,"I think it's about time for us to go to bed, Honey."

29

John had sprawled out on the couch. "Goodnight, you two, "I think I'll wait up for Don."

"Okay son," I replied. Going over to the couch, I bent down and gave him a kiss.

I was awakened by the loud ringing of the phone. As I reached for the receiver, I glanced at the clock. *Who*, I thought, *could possibly be calling us at 2:30 a.m.*

"Hello."

"Dad, this is Bill . . . I . . . I just received a call from the Washington State Patrol. They've found Don's old Pontiac station wagon. It was involved in an accident about an hour ago. Because it was registered in David's name, they called here. Do you know who could have been driving it? They didn't find any identification on the driver."

My heart was in my throat and I could hardly speak. "I uh . . . I'm quite sure it was Don." Filled with a cold fear, I desperately hoped that I was wrong—that Don wasn't the driver. Finally, I managed to ask, "Was the driver . . . uh . . . badly hurt?"

"The driver, whoever it was, died in the crash. Dad," Bill suggested, clutching at straws, "maybe it wasn't Don, maybe someone else was using the wagon."

"No!" I shouted in anguish. "It's not fair! It's not fair! Not another son!"

"Dad, I'll be there as soon as I can!"

Elsie, knowing that something terrible had happened, anxiously asked, "Honey, what is it? What's wrong? Is it Don? Has he been in an accident? Is he hurt?"

When I told her what Bill had told me, she fell prostrate across the bed and began screaming and beating her fists against the bed. I put my arms around her but words of comfort and reassurance weren't there. I knew what she was feeling.

We immediatly awoke John and told him what happened. It was so difficult; they were very close. For several minutes we just sat there in a daze, then, gathering my wits about me as best I could, I said, "I'm going to call the StatePatrol but, before I do, I feel that we should pray together." If ever a prayer was lifted to God with a broken heart to urge it on its way, it was my appeal to Jesus that terrible night—"Jesus, we implore You to uphold us and give us strength. We're not sure what has happened. Please, Jesus, hold us in Your loving arms . . ."

Before I could get to the phone to call, the doorbell rang. Quickly opening the door, I was confronted by three uniformed officers—two Franklin County Deputies and a Washington State Patrol Officer. After identifying themselves, one of the deputies asked, "Are you Mr. Cole?"

"Yes, I am. Will you please come in?"

They followed me into the living room. It was obvious that they were uncomfortable and were trying to keep what they were feeling insulated behind their badges. "Mr. Cole," the State Patrol Officer asked, "do you, or does someone in your family, own a 1965 Pontiac station wagon?"

"Yes, it belongs to my son, Donald; but, it's registered to another son, David, who is deceased." When they looked puzzled, I explained how, after David's death three years earlier, I had given the car to Donald and that he had never gotten around to transferring the title into his name.

"Sir, I hate to tell you this, but the driver of that Pontiac failed to negotiate a turn at the intersection where Argent Road becomes Argent Street. The car left the road and crashed into a residence. A fire started." He hesitated. "The driver was trapped in the car—pinned behind the wheel. Regretfully, before he could be removed, he died of smoke inhalation. Could it have been your son who was driving the wagon?"

I heard my voice, but couldn't recognize it as mine, "Yes, I'm certain it was," I whispered, barely able to speak as my voice broke with emotion. "Was anyone with him? What about the people in the house?"

"No, he was alone. And, fortunately, the residents of the

31

home were all in their bedrooms at the other end of the house away from the crash area."

"There's little doubt that it was Don," I said, breaking down and burying my face in my hands.

"Presumably so," the deputy said gently. "The body has been taken to Greenly Funeral Home. Mr. Cole, could you meet me there at 9:00 in the morning?"

"Of course."

As the officers prepared to leave, although sincere in their expressions of sympathy, I sensed that they hadn't told us everything about the accident and was grateful for their tact in sparing us the more gruesome aspects.

Soon after Bill telephoned, Elsie called our pastors. Now, as the officers were getting into their cars, Pastor Strong drove up the driveway, followed a few minutes later by Pastor Foster. The prayer support they provided was most welcome and helped soothe our broken hearts.

After they left, John, Elsie, and I remained awake the entire night talking and trying to comfort one another. During that long, dark period I called Michael and other family members to let them know the dreadful news. Later that morning, when I reached Paula in California, it was difficult to tell her that the father of her children, the man she had shared a significant part of her life with, was gone.

Our newspaper was delivered about 8:00 a.m. In it, on the front page, was a description of the accident. The article struck me as being couched in journalese language and insensitive. However, because my heart was filled with so much pain, I realized that I was probably being overly harsh in my judgment. It's hard to be objective when it's your loved one they are talking about.

Pastor Strong drove with me to the funeral home where the funeral director, deputy, and the Franklin County Coroner were waiting for me to arrive.

"Mr. Cole," the coroner said softly, "we're sorry that you

had to come, but we need positive identification that it is your son."

"I understand. Don has brown curly hair . . ." I began.

The coroner, interrupting me gently, asked, "Is this your son's shoe?"

My head dropped into my hands and my entire body shook with emotion. Pastor Strong held me in a firm embrace. My fears had been realized—a physical description would do the coroner no good in the identification process. Not a body—a shoe. *How could I possibly tell his precious mother!*

After what seemed like two or three minutes, I looked up and nodded, then indicated that the "love beads" were a more positive identification. The beads, given to him by Brandy, were strung on a small safety pin and fastened to the shoe laces.

Our sons, Bill and Michael, arrived by noon on Wednesday. *How difficult it was for them!* We did our best to console one another.

The following day Elsie and I had to drive to the mortuary to make the funeral arrangements for yet another son. We selected the casket and arranged for our son to be buried next to David. Elsie and I had already made arrangements for the day when God would call us home: our earthly bodies would be buried on the other side of David's grave.

I was determined to find out exactly what had happened on that fateful morning of the crash. John obtained a great deal of information from his friends and I gathered some additional information from friends who lived nearby and had visited the scene shortly after the crash.

Don, as we assumed, had gone to spend the evening with a friend. After leaving his friend's house, for some unknown reason, he drove two or three miles to Pasco where he was stopped by a sheriff's deputy who had spotted him hurriedly leaving a parking lot. After stopping Don, the officer returned to his patrol car to radio for Don's driving record, a standard procedure. Don, no doubt convinced his return to California would be delayed, made a mistake—a grievous mistake—he panicked and drove off in an attempt to elude the officer. The officer pursued at a high rate of speed.

Why? The officer had Don's name, license number, and a description of the car. With this information, he could have quickly obtained the data that he needed to apprehend Don. This was proven by how rapidly they were able to contact Bill after the accident. True, the officer no doubt believed that Don was attempting to flee from a serious crime because of his action. Nevertheless, it is my firm belief and the belief of many, including numerous law enforcement officers, that a high speed chase by police, in most instances, is not necessary. Don's case exemplifies why. In saying this, I am not trying to absolve my son of any guilt or blame—he was wrong for leaving the scene and trying to avoid arrest. I would, however, be less than an ardent father if I failed to point out that he might be alive today if the officer had exercised more prudent judgment.

Don headed west toward home and, desperate to elude the officer, turned off his headlights, still continuing at a high rate of speed. After the officer had pursued him three or four miles, Don succeeded in losing him. Unfortunately, with his lights off, he didn't see the curve ahead and crashed into the residence. The crash was horrendous. The car hit with such force that it tore a gaping hole in the side of the house and penetrated well into the kitchen and dining area. Don, pinned in the crumpled, tangled mass of steel, was unable to escape.

It is very likely that, at least initially, he was mercifully rendered unconscious and probably remained that way for at least a short period of time. We never learned whether anyone attempted to free him from the wreckage before the rescue team arrived. I was told that the kitchen area burst into flames just as the team came on the scene. One member of the rescue team reported that Don was shouting for help and frantically attempting to free himself as flames engulfed him and smoke filled the interior of the car.

Unfortunately, the firefighters had not yet arrived. If only they had been called sooner! If only the fire trucks had arrived a few minutes earlier! If only . . . ! The rescue team, at the risk of their own lives, did everything humanly possible to free Don; but, the intense heat forced them to abandon their efforts. The battle was lost, but not because of lack of determination. Those who worked to rescue my son could not have been more valiant.

Later that day, I met my brother Bill at the airport. He had flown in from his home in Youngtown, Arizona. As I shared the circumstances of Donald's death, we were overwhelmed with emotion and clung to one another for support. Bill and Valerie, his wife, had no children, and always looked upon our sons with favor—loving them as though they were their own.

The next morning as we sat at the breakfast table, I said, "The people in the Tri-Cities should know the true and complete story about Don!"

Elsie agreed. "Yes, that newspaper article only told one side of the story."

I turned to my brother, "Bill, would you like to ride over to Kennewick with me so I can have a talk with the editor of the newspaper?"

"For sure," Bill answered. "I wouldn't miss it!"

When we arrived at the newspaper office, I asked to speak to the editor and was ushered into his office. After introducing myself and Bill, I told him I wanted the true story behind my son's character and his tragic death made known to the public. He was very cooperative and, to my surprise, said that if I would write such an article for the paper that he would print it. He was true to his word and the following day my article, *A Father Remembers His Son*, appeared in the newspaper:

A Father Remembers His Son

On Sept. 14, 1983, at approximately 1:40 a.m., our beloved son, Donald Lee Cole, was taken from us as a result of an automobile accident.

Don was a handsome young man, extremely talented in music, personable and pleasant with nearly a constant smile. He was exceptionally devoted to his two daughters, his parents and his brothers, all of whom are as equally devoted to him. We are and have always been a very close family.

Don's older brother, our beloved David, was killed in a motorcycle accident three years ago near Spokane.

Don loved life and enjoyed so many pleasures of life. His plans for the future included a position with the California Fish and Game Department; with which he had previously been associated and he was to take a Civil Service exam on Sept. 24. Don and I had been together all of Tuesday, September 13. He had told me of his plans to follow the Civil Service position but also to pursue his music in which he was extremely talented. I encouraged him to do so as I am confident he would have been successful as he was not only talented but very intelligent with a handsome physique.

Don had moved from California less than three years ago. At first, conditions were quite good for him economically and with his wife and family, but during the past years conditions deteriorated. He was divorced from his wife, lost his job and his pickup was stolen. His former wife returned to California with the children. Being separated from the children was most difficult for him. His personal belongings were few and included his clothing, his personal effects and his old Pontiac station wagon.

He had been employed last winter and spring but was laid off at the beginning of the summer and was currently drawing unemployment compensation. He was temporarily living with us and was as happy as one could be under the circumstances.

After his California driver's license expired, he failed to obtain a Washington driver's license. He had three or four traffic violations, but nothing major, and, as a result, seldom drove. Other than for these traffic problems, Don had always been a model citizen, having never been arrested or charged with a crime of any sort. He had served in the Navy and was given an honorable discharge.

The day before his death, Don had been happy, cheerful and looking forward to his trip to California the following week to take the Civil Service exam and to be with his darling daughters— Brandy (8) and Courtney (5). He had had a pleasant day and had visited with some friends for a couple of hours that evening.

What led to his tragic death one can only assume. No doubt when he was stopped by the sheriff's patrolman, he was fearful of being detained and unable to complete his plans of going to California the following week. A high-speed chase ensued and where Argent Road ends and sharply turns into Argent Street across Road 100, he failed to negotiate the curve, crashing into the Clapper residence.

We are so thankful that none of the Clapper family was injured.

The grief, pain and sorrow are almost unbearable, but we are Christians and we know that God will sustain us.

Bob Cole
Devoted Father of Donald Lee Cole
Pasco

On the day before the funeral, Elsie and I stood in front of a closed casket. "Oh Honey, it's so hard to bid good-bye to Don and not be able to see him," Elsie cried.

"Oh God, give us strength to bear this burden," I prayed.

37

The church was filled to capacity for the funeral service. A tape of *Sisters* was played during the service and there was not a dry eye in the sanctuary. It was so difficult to look upon the closed casket, unable to view our son, to give him a final touch, a final kiss, a final glimpse.

Don was interred beside David. Once again our hearts were torn as we expressed our final farewell. I held Elsie close. "Honey, we're placing his body beside David's, but we can take comfort in knowing that they're not here—they're rejoicing together in Heaven."

About two weeks after the funeral, John asked, "Why don't you two still take that trip to Vancouver, B.C. that you had planned?"

"He's right Elsie, now is as good a time as any. We should go."

Elsie agreed and helped me prepare our camper for the trip. The following day we were on our way to Vancouver.

"Elsie," I asked, as we were driving down the freeway. "Do you remember how proud we were when Don won first place with his accordion solo in the music contest at Spokane?"

"Of course! Who could forget those big brown eyes and beaming smile when he turned to us with pride and delight as he accepted his award. We were so happy for him! So proud!"

Without putting our thoughts into words, Elsie and I knew we were going through a period of detached mourning when our eyes would suddenly become misty and a word would catch in our throats with a sudden memory of David or Don.

We were passing through a recovery stage whereby the mind accepts the presence of a deep wound that requires gentle healing, but the heart continues to overflow with sadness and must cry out or drown in its grief.

As we drove along, I thought of a verse from the Book of Revelation: *"And God shall wipe away all tears from their eyes; and there shall be no more death, neither sorrow, nor crying, neither shall there be any more pain."* (Revelation 21:4)

CHAPTER THREE

Tears of Sorrow—Tears of Joy

John was glad to see us when we returned from Vancouver and told us how lonely he felt while we were gone. That evening, while we were making plans for an upcoming fishing trip, he admitted that he was depressed over Don's death.

Don had planned to help him refurbish the interior of his van. Much to John's delight, I volunteered to help in Don's place. We spent several busy days measuring, purchasing materials, and installing an engine cover, carpeting, a sleeping bed, water tank, basin, and a bench seat. When we were finished, his van was a beauty to behold.

It was while we were fishing that a shadow crossed John's face, and he told me that he was recovering from a deep depression. His depression had been apparent to his mother and me, causing us great concern.

"You know Dad, during the time I was temporarily working away from home, I was at my lowest level. Once I had to fight an impulse to drive my own vehicle into the path of an eighteen-wheeler."

When he shared this passing fantasy of suicide with me, it felt as though an angel of darkness had suddenly dimmed the sun.

"John, everyone at some point in their lives experiences thoughts of self destruction."

He seemed relieved. "What does it mean?"

"Usually such thoughts are a sign that the person is temporarily weary and in need of a fresh outlook—a new perspective on life—one that takes their thoughts away from themselves. You've lost two brothers; this kind of terrible grief is an extremely difficult burden to bear. Just remember that I am here for you—we all are!"

I was concerned about what he had told me and silently vowed that I would do everything in my power to help brighten his pathway and ease his burden.

John, our youngest, was slow in physical development, only reaching a height of 5' 9" and a maximum weight of 145 pounds. In our intimate family circle, we affectionately called him "Little John." A handsome young man with a comely beard, he—even though they would never admit it—became the envy of his older married brothers. *Why?* Because the sexual revolution that swept the country had reached its peak during his late teens and he was looked upon with favor by a multitude of females. He was single, available and willing.

Because of a reading disability, John never did as well scholastically as his brothers, causing him to have feelings of inferiority. He completed high school and, having no interest in pursuing a higher education, enlisted in the Navy shortly after graduation. For years he had heard his Uncle Bill speak about how much he had enjoyed being in the Navy and looked forward to living the life of a sailor. Unfortunately, because of his reading disability, he was given an early discharge. This was a compound blow to his self worth and ego.

We loved him and understood his sensitivity. His less endowed abilities to cope in a competitive world made us very protective. After all, he was the baby of the family.

Later, when I recalled my discussion with John about suicide, my thoughts were turned to my own mental combat. I remembered something Elsie and I had discussed when we were on our trip to Vancouver. Struggling with the deaths of my two boys, I kept referring over and over again to Harold Kuchner's book *When Bad Things Happen To Good People*. His words were helpful at a time when, no matter how hard I tried, I couldn't make any sense out of their deaths. Kuchner's writings helped me to better understand my relationship with God and that He would not hold me accountable for my sons' deaths. He wrote:

> God does not cause our misfortunes. Some are caused by bad luck, some are caused by bad people, and some are simply an inevitable consequence of our being human and being mortal, living in a world of inflexible natural law. The painful things that happen to us are not punishment for our misbehavior, nor are they in any way a part of some grand design on God's part. Because the tragedy is not God's will, we need not feel hurt or betrayed by God when tragedy strikes. We can turn to Him for help in overcoming it. Precisely because we can tell ourselves that God is as outraged by it as we.
>
> Does that mean that my suffering has no meaning? This is the most significant challenge that can be offered to the point of view I have been advocating in the book. We could bear nearly any pain or disappointment if we thought there was a reason behind it, a purpose to it. But even a lesser burden becomes too much for us if we feel it makes no sense.

Even though I resisted doing so, I finally came to agree with another of Kuchner's observations:

> The facts of life and death are neutral. We, by our responses, give suffering either a positive or a negative meaning. Illnesses, accidents, human tragedies kill people. But they do not necessarily kill life or faith. If the death and suffering of someone we love makes us bitter, jealous, against all religion, and incapable of happiness, we turn the person who dies into one of the "devils martyrs." If suffering and death in someone close to us brings us to explore the limits of our capacity for strength and love and cheerfulness, if it leads us to discover sources of consolation we never knew before, then we make the person into a witness for the affirmation of life rather than its rejection.

Copyright © 1981 by Harold S. Kushner.
Copyright © 1989 by Harold S. Kushner. Reprinted by permission of Schocken Books, distributed by Pantheon Books, a division of Random House, Inc.

Viewed with a positive perspective, I thought, *the death of our sons could make them witnesses for the affirmation of the lives of those they left behind.* It was a good thought; but it didn't diminish my sense of emptiness or take away my feeling of loss. An extension of myself—my blood and tissue,—my spirit,—had been cut off from me. And yet, in spite of that observation, I recognized the "emptiness" as a challenge and knew that it had to be filled with something. That "something" was knowing that my sons were still very much alive and in a far better place. I had no idea why their lives ended at such an early age; however, my faith gave me the strength to believe that the reasons were known, but only to God. *And who was I to question my omnipotent, omniscient and omnipresent God?*

Shortly after John went to work as a mechanic for the Tri-City Herald, he brought a girl home that he had told us he was seriously interested in. "Hi, Mom! Hi Dad!" he called out as they got out of his truck. "This is Marilyn."

Marilyn was quite pleasant. An attractive blonde who, as we chatted, warmly entered into the conversation. However, from the very beginning, Elsie and I felt that she was not the right girl for John. We could sense that she wasn't being totally sincere with him about their relationship and felt that he should seek out a girl who, not only was attractive, but also stable, secure, and sincere. Sometimes, parents are hard to please!

Eventually, John said, "Hate to cut off all this stimulating conversation, but we have a video to watch tonight. So, if you'll excuse us, we'll be on our way."

Over the next three or four weeks we got to know Marilyn quite well. We still silently disapproved, but were careful not to let her, or John, know it. And, as John shared more and more with us about her raggedy background, we became even more deeply concerned. We sincerely hoped, as John indicated, that Marilyn's life had changed for the better.

It came as no surprise when, a few days before Christmas, they announced their engagement. Marilyn proudly held out her hand, showing us her shining new diamond.

Smiling, Elsie exclaimed, "How wonderful! We wish you the very best!" Then, quickly getting to her feet, she embraced Marilyn.

"That's great kids. Have you set the date yet?" I asked, joining in their embrace.

"Yes," Marilyn answered, "the most romantic day for a wedding—February 14th—Valentine's Day."

Despite our misgivings about her, the four of us spent a most enjoyable Christmas together, exchanging presents, talking, and enjoying the warmth of the fireplace. John was especially happy. In fact, one could say he was glowing almost

44

as brightly as the embers in the fire. Later, we shared a delicious turkey dinner.

The following morning, Elsie joined me in the living room as I looked over the numerous maps for our upcoming trip to California and Arizona. We thoroughly enjoyed the sunshine of the southland during the winter months and were very much looking forward to the trip. Hesitantly Elsie said, "Honey, I know I probably shouldn't feel this way, but I can't help but wonder if this marriage is going to be good for John. I definitely have reservations about Marilyn being the right girl."

"Honey, I've got reservations, too. However, we can't live his life for him. It's his decision, not ours."

Other than two very brief periods of time, John had spent all 28 years of his entire life at home with us. Elsie and I were both very close to him. John, as our youngest, had always been our baby. As a result, we probably sheltered him more than we should have. We always provided for his needs whenever he was unable to do so; however, he rarely took advantage of us and appreciated all that we did for him.

We desperately wanted him to be successful and worked hard to build his self confidence. To further his education, we persuaded him to enroll in a vocational tech class at a local community college to learn auto body repair and refinishing. Unfortunately, because he was apprehensive about passing the academic studies the course required, he dropped out after only a few weeks.

During the week following Christmas, Elsie and I prepared our camper for our trip south. We expected to be gone for several months and return home sometime around the middle of March. Just in time to begin our spring work on our mini-farm and to keep Uncle Sam happy by filing our income tax return.

On New Year's Day 1986, I asked John, "Son, can you think of anything else you might need while we're away? The freezer is full and the shelves are stocked with everything from applesauce to zucchini."

"No, Pop, I can't. You and mom have thought of every-thing. Walking into the utility room is like walking into a supermarket."

"Son," I said, laughing, "methinks that you do exaggerate a bit." Then, continuing in a more serious tone, "Take good care of things while we're gone and be sure to send our mail to Uncle Bill by the tenth of each month. Hold any mail we get in March until we return. Please don't drive my car unless it's absolutely necessary and under no circumstances are you to allow anyone else to drive it. Okay?"

"No problem, Pop! I have my new truck, so I won't have any need to drive your car."

"John, can you think of anything else?"

"Nope, I think we've covered everything. But, if I think of anything, I'll call you."

Bright and early the next morning, January 2, 1986, Elsie and I pulled out of our driveway and headed the camper south. John stood just inside the garage door waving good-bye.

It was while we were in Arizona visiting my brother Bill that we got a distress call from John. "Honey," I suggested to Elsie, "why don't you pick up on the other phone."

"Hello, Son, what's wrong?"

"Marilyn and I have broken up," he began. I could tell by the tone of his voice that he was upset and depressed. "She can't seem to make up her mind about what she really wants!" Then, while Elsie and I listened, he spent the next fifteen or twenty minutes telling us about everything that led up to their breakup.

"Son, from what you're saying, it sounds as though she wants everything her way and doesn't want to compromise or give anything back. I know it would be hard for you to do, but you might want to consider dropping her completely. Think about it! You might be better off. By the way, has she returned the ring you gave her?"

"Yes, a couple of days ago. I asked her to give it back." The way he said it, I knew that he was upset about what I had said.

Even though we talked for at least another five minutes, when I hung up the phone, I was still apprehensive about his state of mind. *What*, I thought, *has Marilyn done to him*?

Elsie joined me in telling Bill about what was going on. We decided to give the problem to God, so we prayed. When we had finished, I felt a strong urgency to call John back, and did so at once. "John, you need to talk to someone in person about what has happened and how you feel. Please," I implored, "promise me that you'll go see Pastor Strong or Pastor Foster! You need the counseling that they can give at this time. Okay?"

"Oh, I don't know . . . I'll be okay," he replied unconvincingly.

Despite being extremely busy for the next several days with pruning, trimming, and other yard work—something I did for Bill every winter when we came to visit—we all felt concern for John. I enjoyed helping Bill do the things around the yard that were too difficult for him to do by himself. We had always been close and regretted that we were unable to spend more time together. I was pleased that we had nearly completed the annual cleanup as we planned on leaving for Yuma in a day or two.

Elsie and I, even while visiting relatives and friends, preferred to sleep in our camper. Early the next morning, we were awakened by Bill loudly rapping on our door. Half asleep, it took me a moment to understand what he was saying. "Bobby, John called about four o'clock. He was all excited. I asked him if he could wait until later and call back. He agreed. Said he'd call back at six. It's nearly six now, you'd better get dressed and come on into the house."

We hurriedly dressed and waited for his call—a call that never came. Finally, at eight o'clock, knowing that something had to be wrong, I called him. He answered right away, "Okay, Son, what's wrong?" I could tell from the ensuing pause that he was reluctant to tell me something.

"I have some bad news, Pop," he said with hesitation. "I was in a bind yesterday. Marilyn was here and had no way of getting to work. I couldn't take her as I had to be at work myself within a few minutes. I felt I had no choice but to let her use your car. She promised that she'd be careful and drive straight to and from the restaurant with no stops in between. But she lied. Instead of coming home after work, she went to a bar and got loaded. Then, on the way home . . . she rear-ended another car, totaling your car and causing considerable damage to the other. Pop, I'm sorry."

After catching my breath, I asked, "Son, was Marilyn or anyone else hurt?"

"Marilyn had some minor injuries, but nothing serious. She was treated in the emergency room and released. The police immediately took her to jail. Thankfully, no one in the other car was hurt."

"That's great! Most important though, John, how are you?"

"I'm doing okay, but I feel so bad about your car."

"John, it's only a car and can be replaced. I'm concerned about you. Do you think we should come home?"

"No, I'm okay. Don't change your plans, Pop. I'll be fine."

After hanging up, still apprehensive about John's state of mind, I turned to Elsie, "Honey, what do you think, should we return home now or go ahead with our itinerary?"

"I'm not sure; you spoke with him. What do you think we should do?"

"Let's go on to San Diego and make up our minds before leaving there."

Two days later we left the hospitality of my brother's home. It was late afternoon when we pulled into a suitable RV park in Yuma. After setting up the camper for our overnight stay, I sought out a pay phone and called John. Although still depressed, I could tell that his mood had improved. He voice sounded even more positive when I said, "Remember our plans to open a mini-mart, Son!"

"I'm looking forward to it!"

"Good! Have you talked to Pastor Strong or Foster yet?"

"No, but I'll be okay."

"Please do!" I implored.

Slowly, walking back to the camper, I silently prayed, *Heavenly Father, please take care of John.*

We spent two days in San Diego, visiting the Zoo and Sea World. The following day we headed north to Moro Bay where we parked our camper in a state campground located but a stone's throw from the mighty and beautiful Pacific Ocean.

After spending five days at Moro Bay, I turned to Elsie and said, "Honey, I'm far too concerned about John. Let's leave for home in the morning."

"I'm with you Darling; we can't get home any too soon to suit me!"

On the way we stopped for a couple of days in Bend, Oregon to visit with our son Michael. From there, we drove straight home and arrived in Pasco in the early afternoon— tired but glad to be home.

John was delighted that we were home. "Gosh, but I'm sure glad to see you guys!" he said with emotion as he hugged each of us.

"And we're glad to see you, too, Honey!" Elsie said. "We've been worried about you. Let's go inside so you can fill us in on everything that's happened since we've been gone."

Let's take a look at you, son," I said, stepping back and holding him by the arms. "You look exhausted and it's obvious that you've lost weight. Haven't you been eating?"

"Not much, Pop. My appetite hasn't been too good and I've had trouble sleeping."

"Don't worry, Son. I'll put that meat back on your bones

in a hurry," Elsie said.

"You can if anyone can, Mom. I've really been looking forward to some of your great cooking."

After we went inside, John spoke in great detail about Marilyn's behavior, ridiculous demands, and deep sense of insecurity.

"Is she still in jail?" I asked.

"Yes, but she's supposed to get out tomorrow. The last time I talked to her she said that she had left some things here and would probably come by and pick them up. I hope she doesn't come; I really don't want to see her again."

Shortly after noon the following day, Elsie, John and I backed out of the driveway in John's truck. As we started down the road, John said "Hurry up, Pop. She said she was coming over this afternoon and I don't want to be here if she does." The words were barely out of his mouth when a car passed us coming from the opposite direction. "Oh no, there she is! She's in that car! I guess we'll have to turn around and go back."

A few moments later we pulled back into our driveway and parked alongside the car in which Marilyn was a passenger. We greeted her as warmly as we could but, under the circumstances, Elsie and I found it difficult to be civil. However, not wanting to say or do anything that might upset John, we forced ourselves to be courteous.

Marilyn apparently had no remorse, regret, sense of guilt or shame for the many complications she had either created, or been involved in, that affected John. She spoke with frivolity, brushing aside her jail sentence and the wrecking of our car as matters of little consequence. I realized, but could say nothing to John, that his attraction for her was almost entirely physical.

After returning from church on Sunday, February 16, hoping to find an affordable replacement for my demolished car, I sat down to check out the classified section of the newspaper.

When I was done, I called out to Elsie, "Honey, I've found two or three that sound pretty good and are in our price range. Want to go with me to check them out?"

"Sure thing, Hon. Let me fix my face and hair and I'll be right with you!"

We did find a used car to our liking. It belonged to a rather elderly lady who agreed that my son could take it for a test drive. After dinner that evening I asked John, the mechanic of our family, if he would check it out for us the next day. He agreed, then dropped something totally unexpected on us. "I'm going to run over to Marilyn's place in Kennewick and see if I can collect some money that she owes me. I shouldn't be out too late, but don't wait up for me."

"John," Elsie exclaimed, "I'm surprised! You said you weren't going to see her again."

"Just this once," John replied, as he closed the door.

After he left, I turned to Elsie and said uneasily, "I hope he doesn't regret going over there."

The next day, before leaving to check out the car, John only casually mentioned his visit with Marilyn. When he returned from the test drive, he gave me a good report. "Pop, I drove the car around and looked it over real good. It's in top condition for a low mileage four-year-old car. If I were you, I'd buy it!"

Taking his advice, I bought it that very afternoon.

The next day was to be a day that is marked forever in our family memories. John returned from a trip to Kennewick accompanied by Marilyn who was visibly intoxicated. "Marilyn came with me to get her things," John said defensively, as he entered the house.

Neither Elsie nor I commented as they went by us and down the stairs leading to his apartment.

"Honey, I don't want her around here," Elsie complained in a loud whisper.

"I know; I feel the same way. That girl is tearing John

51

apart, and he can't seem to free himself from her."

"Why did she have to come back up here? Why didn't she stay in Texas?" Elsie asked with feeling. "It's clear that she's only interested in herself and her own well-being. Why, with all the girls in the Tri-Cities area to choose from, did he have to pick her? Maybe, he doesn't want to hurt her, or maybe he's so blinded by his feelings that he can't see that she's just using him. He told me that he had been wanting to get married and have children as his brothers have, but why hurry? He's only 28!"

And so we talked for some time about John's trying situation.

Later, John came upstairs and asked, "Pop, can you lend me five dollars? I'd like to rent a video for tonight."

Before I could control my tongue, I replied tersely, "You mean you're going to allow her to spend the evening?" Even as I spoke, I was reaching for my billfold.

Elsie spoke up, "John, open your eyes. Can't you see what she's doing to you? She's going to break your heart!"

Handing him the five dollar bill, I reinforced what Elsie had just told him. "Son, the last time we talked about this, you emphatically said that you had no intentions of seeing her again, and yet she's here. John, she's no good for you? Can't you see that she's causing you nothing but trouble?"

"Pop, we just want to spend this one last time together," John replied brusquely.

"Okay," Elsie stated firmly, "but after tonight, I don't want her around here anymore."

"After all, Son, this is our home," I said, as John turned to go downstairs.

"You mean, this isn't my home, too?"

Realizing I should have referred to ownership rather than domicile, I said, "John, you know you may live here as long as you want."

"Well, that does it!" John shouted from his apartment door.

"I had wanted to assure him that our house was his home, but he didn't hear. *Oh well*, I thought, *I'll tell him later . . .*

Coming from the kitchen, Elsie entered the living room where I was reading. "Honey, " she said, I hate to bother you, but the water's been running downstairs for quite some time. Surely, no one would be taking such a long shower. Maybe something's wrong."

"No problem, I'll check on it."

I rapped on the apartment door and listened, but no one answered. Not wanting to disturb John's privacy, I decided to return to the living room. I had barely picked up the magazine I was reading and sat down when Marilyn bolted up the stairwell screaming, "Help! Oh, God, Help! It's John!" She was so hysterical that, for a moment, I had difficulty understanding what she was saying. Finally, she calmed down enough to say, "He . . . he's in the bathroom!"

Quickly I ran downstairs. I was horrified by what I saw in the bathroom and, in fear and shock, stood transfixed, my mind refusing to accept what my eyes told me was real— *John had hung himself*!

I fought against the agony, the despair, the feeling of near collapse. Fortunately, I had been trained in CPR, and knew that it was imperative that I put my feelings on hold and take immediate action. *John needs me*, I thought, *I can't allow myself to be overcome by my emotions. I only hope it's not too late*!

I heard Elsie gasp behind me and, turning around, saw that she, too, was near collapse; her eyes filled with fright and disbelief. Shock had taken her voice away. Marilyn, still semi-hysterical, was standing behind her.

"Marilyn," I shouted, "get control of yourself! Go call 911!" She didn't move. "Marilyn, do you understand? Go call 911! Now!"

"Yes," she replied weakly, still not moving.

"Now!" I shouted again. Finally it registered and she

ran down the hall to make the call.

John was hanging from the shower head by his bathrobe belt. I lifted his limp body and attempted to untie the knot, but it was too tight. "Elsie, hurry! Get me a sharp knife from the kitchen." She responded immediately. It was obvious that she would do anything she possibly could to help me in my feeble attempts to sustain life in our precious son. Continuing to lift John's body to relieve the pressure on his neck, I prayed while waiting for her to return.

With the knife, I quickly cut the belt, lowered John to the floor and, after hurriedly instructing Elsie as to how she could assist, began administering CPR. She bravely followed my every instruction.

Why isn't he responding? Oh God, how I wanted to see some sign of life. There wasn't any! However, determined to do all we could, we continued our life saving efforts. Many thoughts rushed through my mind. *Why would he want to commit suicide? He's so young and has so much to live for. The pressures of life couldn't have been that great, could they? He must have thought they were! But extreme enough to take his own life? No way! Why did he turn on the water in the tub? Did he turn it on assuming that Marilyn would hear it and come to check on him? Did he turn it on in an effort to get her attention? Or was it turned on accidently?* I prayed! Oh, God, how I prayed! And through her tears, I knew that Elsie was praying, too.

After what seemed an eternity, a sheriff's deputy arrived and took over. I took Elsie's place and we continued to administer CPR. Checking John's vital signs, we found a faint pulse. *Thank You, God,* I thought, *for this ray of hope!*

Marilyn, after calling 911, remained hysterical, crying and shouting over and over, "It's my fault! All my fault!"

Inwardly, I felt perhaps it was, but I rebuked any further thought. "Elsie, call the church and ask the pastors to come over right away."

Finally, a fully equipped ambulance arrived. Survival techniques using the most modern equipment were employed. Leaving John in the hands of the paramedics, I made my way to the living room where Elsie, in shock and on the verge of complete collapse, was sitting on the couch. Taking her in my arms, I, too, felt my system go numb with shock. While I was busy administering CPR, my mind was too occupied to fully comprehend what had happened; but, now that I had relaxed slightly, my emotions had kicked in and I felt like I was going to totally lose it. *But I can't*, I thought, *Elsie and John need me!*

One of the paramedics came to the top of the stairway to tell me they were leaving to take John to the hospital. Pastor Strong, who had arrived only minutes before, asked us to ride with him to the hospital. We prayed all the way to the hospital, asking God to intervene and spare John's life.

After providing the emergency room personnel with the essential information they needed, we sat in the waiting room to begin what would seem to be an endless wait. I placed my arm around my dear wife and held her close. *Was it for her support and comfort? Or mine?*

As the doctor somberly entered the waiting room, I somehow sensed that what we were about to hear would be what we had feared the most. "Mr. and Mrs. Cole?" he said approaching us. "Mr. and Mrs. Cole," he repeated, "I'm sorry! We did everything we could, but we were unable to revive your son. He's gone!"

His words echoed in my mind as I thought, *No, God! Not another son! Why God, why? Why did you let him die? It's not fair, God! It's not fair!* The emotional dam that I had so carefully built, burst, and tears of sorrow coursed down my cheeks. All hope was gone! I was deep in the valley of despair! My wife, too, was in that same valley.

As soon as we arrived home, I called Bill and Michael. Bill said he would leave within the hour and Michael said he would come the following morning. Later, a sheriff's deputy came to ask us about the circumstances surrounding John's death. He, too, believed that John could have succumbed to a self-induced accident as a result of an attempt to gain Marilyn's attention.

Pastor Strong, Pastor Foster and a number of friends stayed with us until Bill arrived that evening. We were grateful for their company and support.

That night, our pillows were saturated with tears of sorrow as my darling wife and I spent the entire night without sleep. I softly whispered, "Elsie . . . Sweetheart, I'm not sure that I'm going to make it. Losing three of our precious children in a period of six years is just too much to bear."

"I know, Honey. Life will be unbearable without him. He's lived here with us nearly his entire life. Oh, God, how I miss him! Oh, God, how I love him!"

Michael arrived early the next morning. He and Bill, our two remaining sons, gave us strength throughout the day. We were blessed with visits from many caring friends and relatives. Even so, nothing they could say or do could ease the pain of our broken hearts. Tears flowed constantly; our voices were weak and broken; sleep escaped us. We tried to come to grips with the reality that John's life on earth had truly ended but it was so hard to believe. Reality can be so painful!

Once again we stood beside a casket to bid farewell to yet another of our dear sons. Elsie and I were so weak that we could barely stand. Bill and Michael escorted us to the casket to bid their brother a final farewell—to give him a final touch, a final kiss, a final glimpse.

"He looks serene, docsn't he, Darling?" I whispered to Elsie.

"Oh, yes, Honey, he does. He looks as though he's cast away all the cares, trials, and troubles of this world and is free at last. And, he is! He's free! He's running free with his brothers in the blessed Kingdom of God."

As she spoke, I remembered how John had come rushing into our bedroom late one evening with tears glistening in his big brown eyes and a glowing smile on his face to tell us how, after viewing a Billy Graham video with his friends, he had invited Jesus into his life.

John's funeral filled the church to capacity. Many of those in attendance at the funeral were his friends—young people who had come to love and respect him for the good, kind, and generous person that he was.

We buried John beside David on a bitterly cold day in February in one of the lots that we had reserved for ourselves. To be close to our sons when our own lives ended, Elsie and I made arrangements for "double-decking" in the remaining lot. As cold as it was that day, we lingered at the graveside after the service ended. It was so very difficult to bring ourselves to the final farewell.

Not long after the funeral, I said to Elsie, "Darling, I keep listening for the apartment door to open and expect him, at any moment, to come bounding up the stairs asking, 'what's for dinner?' Can't you see his big smile and the twinkle in his eyes?"

"Yes, Honey, I certainly can," she replied, struggling with a flood of tears.

About two weeks after his death I was home alone thinking about John and his death when an overwhelming burden of guilt threatened to consume me. I couldn't help but feel that I was somewhat responsible for John taking his life. *Is it possible*, I thought, *that when I reminded John that he was living in our home, I pushed him over the edge? Had my remark increased his depression to the point that it triggered his suicide? Why couldn't I have recognized his mental and emotional stability and not spoken those words? If only I had observed his reaction more closely and followed him to his apartment and talked with him, reasoned with him, and stayed with him until the suicidal moment passed. If only I could have those few minutes back.* "Oh, God," I cried out in torment, "Why didn't you open my eyes to see what was happening?"

My oppression became as an active volcano, flowing a lava of guilt over my island of despair. I couldn't sleep and had to obtain a prescription for sleeping pills from my doctor. The pills brought about sleep but usually, after sleeping for only one or two hours, I would awaken wide-eyed for the remainder of the night, my head flooded with thoughts of *why, if only,* and *what if.* I lost weight and would burst into tears for no apparent cause. My voice and demeanor became weak and broken.

With resolution, I finally threw the pills away and placed my burden on Christ. I was determined, with His help, to bring control back into my life and find comfort for my burdened soul.

As I began to read various books on death, my faith was strengthened as I inwardly accepted the fact that God, in His infinite wisdom, could call any of his children home at any time.

Professional writers all seemed to agree that many parents blame themselves when their child is ill or hurt in an accident. *This has to be my fault*, they think. *I failed to do something or did something I should not have done.* They ask, *What if? Why didn't I? How could I have been so careless?* The self-accusations go on and on, causing added pain, and slowing down the healing process. Regretfully, some parents assume this guilt for the rest of their lives. They search themselves, trying to unmask the sin within that they feel must have brought about the sorrowful circumstances. Although all of us are sinners, it is a falsehood to believe that God punishes our children or loved ones because of our sins.

Parents need to understand that their children belong to God—they are on loan to them. The Lord entrusts children to their earthly parents for 18 or 20 years of training and guidance. The loving relationship between parent and child doesn't change once the child becomes an adult—but the parents' obligations do. Although difficult to prepare for, we must be willing to let go of our children when they become adults. Even more difficult, we must give them back to God should He decide to take them home!

With this deeper sense of understanding, I dropped to my knees in front of my chair and, once again, placed my burden at the feet of Jesus. When I arose, there was a joy in my soul and a song in my heart.

Some time later, on a gorgeous day in the month of May, I was returning from Kennewick, slowly cruising on the highway along the Columbia River. I was contemplating the wondrous works of God as I looked upon the fleecy, white clouds that floated in the otherwise clear, blue skies. There were a variety of flowers blooming along the roadside and in the meadows. My thoughts turned from God the Father to Jesus' love and how He had so gloriously comforted my heart and brought me out of the depths of despair. I fully recognized that my love for Him and my family, though great, in no way could compare to the great love He has for me. He proved His love when He gave His life on that cruel cross.

For God to give His Son for the redemption of my sins and the sins of all mankind was beyond my comprehension. I had lost three sons and, no matter what the reason, had difficulty comprehending how any father, even God the Father, could willingly give up a son to death. What a wonderful God! *And*, I thought, looking around me, *if He has given us this much beauty here, what is it like in Heaven? How beautiful and glorious it will be when I can once again be with my sons and rejoice with them in eternal bliss.*

I was thankful that God had given them to us, shared them with us, even though their time with us had been so limited. Unfortunately, that old enemy, doubt, arose again in my mind. *Were the boys prepared to meet God? Had Christ received them unto Himself?*

Suddenly, the love of God came flooding through the window of my heart, filling me joy unspeakable. The Holy Spirit spoke to me, clearing revealing His presence as I had never before experienced. My entire being was shaken. I was in awe of God's glorious might and power, completely oblivious of all around me; guided by holy angels. Never before nor since have I experienced such joy and tranquility. I had truly entered the presence of God. I was allowed a glimpse of Heaven: the glory of His Kngdom; the beauty of His presence, my heavenly home. Peace filled my soul as God confirmed the presence of David, Don and John in the Kingdom of Heaven. Tears of joy coursed down my cheeks as I shouted praises of thanksgiving to my Heavenly Father.

This glorious experience was so magnificent that I wanted to continue with the journey to Heaven, to join my sons on the other side. I fully realized the true magnitude and purity of God's love. *How could Heaven be sweeter than this?*

The Holy Spirit gradually returned me to the natural realm. I continued to be bathed in his love as I was made fully aware that my work on earth was not completed; that my story was to be presented in written form telling others of God's boundless love, the comfort He has to offer, and the grace He provides for all who open their hearts to Him.

Christ has changed my life! With my burden lightened and my heart filled with joy, I am willing to allow God to guide me through His blessed will, ever increasingly aware of His wondrous works, and looking forward to the promise that awaits me in the beauty of Heaven.

CHAPTER FOUR

Death Was No Stranger

When I was young, and even as I grew older, I refused to allow myself to feel that my parents were anything but immortal. Then, when my mother suffered a fatal heart attack, I was shocked beyond belief. Her death was sudden, without warning. At the time she was hospitalized, there was no indication that she had a heart problem.

Mother was a true saint of God, always ministering to others. Even while she was in the hospital she ministered to the needs of the other patients in her room, concerned about their spiritual and physical well being. She died rather prematurely at age 69.

Two years later, my 75 year old father followed her in death. He was lost without mother and had a great deal of difficulty trying to adjust to his loss. He, like my mother, suffered a massive heart attack; however, even though he lived nearly two years more, his passing was just as difficult to bear. From the very inception of his illness, he told me that he was ready to go home and be with her.

Elsie's father died while she was in her teens, while her

mother, a very dear lady, remained in good health until the last days of her life and lived to see her 93rd birthday. Even though she lived alone for many years after the passing of her husband, she remained happy and contented. She, too, often ministered to the needs of others and, as she lived out the final year of her life in a nursing home, she continued to reach out to her fellow residents.

Throughout our marriage Elsie has been my pillar of strength, particularly during the loss of our sons. I can only hope that I have been as strong in supporting her. As difficult and painful as their deaths were for me, I know that Elsie endured pain beyond belief. She was their mother—the one who had nurtured them in her womb—I could only attempt to try and understand what she was feeling.

Other tragedies also struck our family. In July of 1967, Pam, our daughter in law, and our two grandchildren, Angie, five, and Ricky, three, were visiting with us. Bill, her husband, our oldest son, was in the Army and stationed overseas. Pam, who had just returned from the evening church service, was downstairs in the family room visiting with Elsie. I was doing something that every grandfather loves to do, holding little Angie on my lap and reading her a book. Mike and Don were around the house somewhere, and John and Ricky were outside playing on the carport.

John, in his usual exuberance, burst into the house; Ricky was right behind him. "Mommy, can I have some crackers for me and Ricky?"

"Sure, but not too many." she called upstairs. "Just a handful for each of you."

With crackers in hand, the boys headed back out to the carport to eat their snack.

Every day, Elsie watched Angie and Ricky for Pam while she went to work in a food processing plant. The children knew that there was a hard and fast rule that they were not to go into the street or try to cross it unless an adult were with them.

As I was reading to Angie, I heard a loud sickening thud! Leaping up, I ran to the window, afraid of what I might see. My heart was racing. "Oh God! No!" I shouted, seeing Ricky's still, little body lying in the street.

"What is it, Grandpa?" Angie asked.

"Your brother's been hurt, honey," I said, setting her down and heading as quickly as I could for the front door. Just as I reached the living room, John came flying into the house crying and all excited. "Elsie! Pam!" I shouted. "Hurry! Ricky's been hurt!"

Rushing out the door, I heard someone screaming hysterically. Looking toward the sound, I noticed, some 50 feet up the street, someone standing beside their car. Not stopping to see who it was, I dashed down the street to Ricky's side. As I looked upon the bruised and mangled body of my little grandson, tears came to my eyes. My heart was broken and it was racing so fast I was sure that, at any moment, it would surely stop beating.

In only a matter of seconds, Pam and Elsie were standing by my side, living the horror with me. "Cover him and keep him warm, but don't move him. I'll go call an ambulance," I shouted, already running toward the house.

Assured that an ambulance would be dispatched right away, I rushed back to be with Elsie and Pam. Kneeling on the hard pavement beside the still body of my grandson I knew that there was only one thing I could do for him. "Jesus, touch this little boy . . . touch Ricky . . . my grandson. Please let his injuries not be serious and restore him to the vibrant little bundle of energy we love so much. Oh, Jesus, please help us . . . please . . .!"

The sound of the ambulance siren interrupted my prayer, but I didn't mind. I was thankful they were there. After checking his vital signs, a hurried examination, and some cursory treatment, they placed him in the ambulance and, with flashing lights and siren blaring loudly, rushed him away to the hospital.

Leaving John and Angie in Don and Mike's care, we followed the ambulance to the hospital where the doctors told us that his injuries were critical, and they didn't hold out much hope for his recovery. We maintained an all night vigil.

In the morning, I returned home and called the local chapter of the American Red Cross to request their assistance in getting Bill home on emergency leave. I gave them all the information I had, including his Army mailing address.

Shortly after 4:00 p.m. the following afternoon, Ricky's attending physician walked into the waiting room. Elsie was waiting alone; Pam had stepped out for a few minutes. Taking her hands in his, he said, "I'm sorry, Mrs. Cole, your grandson just died." He then gently held her in his arms as she lay her head on his shoulder and burst into tears.

Later, we learned that Ricky's brain had sustained so much damage that, even if he had survived, he would never have been able to function normally.

The day after his death, I thought about the accident, trying to reconstruct in my mind what had happened. The driver of the car, a neighbor who lived just down the street, apparently didn't see my grandson dart out into the street. It was dusk, the visibility was poor, and Ricky was so small, he just didn't see him. Ricky, dashing into the street, probably became aware of the oncoming car and "froze" in fear. The "thud" that I heard was the impact that threw him more than 30 feet through the air. The driver was in shock and was bedridden for days.

I made several follow-up calls to the Red Cross trying to find out when Bill was coming home, but they didn't know. All they could tell me was that they had sent the request and that it was now up to the Army. They did feel, however, that under the circumstances it would be approved. And it was. Bill arrived that same day. The Army had flown him to Saigon in a fighter plane where he caught a military transport to the United States. As soon as he landed, he phoned to see how Ricky was doing. Tearfully, Pam had to tell him that Ricky's life on earth had ended only hours before. The rest of his trip home was filled with tears, sadness, and pain as he thought of the memories of his little boy and the plans he had for him that would never be.

After the funeral, Bill and I sat in the back yard of his place and talked about the joy that Ricky had brought into the hearts of those who were a part of his short life. *How could I know then that, many years later, I would be consoling my eldest son again, following the deaths of three of his brothers.*

CHAPTER FIVE

Dealing With Grief

Without hesitation, Elsie and I would say that the loss of our children was more difficult to deal with than the loss of our parents. Just as we were a part of our parents, our boys were a part of us. All three of them died under tragic circumstances; however, the cause of death didn't really matter . . . they were gone! And with them went a part of us—a part of our lives.

In an effort to broaden my knowledge and understanding of death and dying, the grief process, and life beyond the grave, I have read extensively since their deaths. Most of that reading has been done in conjunction with the research and study for this book.

Many writers point out that one of life's most heartbreaking experiences is the death of a child. I, as do many other writers, concur wholeheartedly.

Reaction to the death of a loved one may vary widely depending on the circumstances that bring about death. A sudden unexpected death, an accidental death, or death by murder or suicide will probably bring greater anguish than a lingering death due to illness, but not necessarily so.

We are born, grow to adulthood, most of us reproduce, we grow old and we die. Once we are born we are sure to die. This is the natural process of life which we cannot change. Death is a part of and the final stage of life. With these simple truths, we are all familiar; yet, many of us would prefer to avoid talking or thinking about death because it is so morbid and depressing.

There is no way we can avoid grief; it is a certainty. While happiness is a choice, all of us will experience grief. Dealing with grief is both an emotional and physical drain; a painful process, but essential to good health. Unresolved grief can, and very likely will, lead to severe physical, emotional, or mental illness; however, if dealt with properly, it can be overcome.

Even though grief is not considered a mental illness by the professional community, it does carry with it many symptoms of such an illness. Some doctors have estimated that as many as one-fourth of all hospital admissions are, in some way, the result of unresolved grief.

We have all heard the old adage, "Time heals all wounds." *But is it true?* The wounds of grief can be deep and the scars many. How we utilize time in resolving grief is far more important than time itself. Consider Fred Walker, an elderly man, who nearly three years ago lost his wife, Evelyn, to an extended bout with cancer. Her illness was lingering, lasting more than two years. Toward the end, the cancer caused her excruciating pain.

As the cancer progressed, Evelyn became more and more dependent on her husband. Fred was reluctant to relinquish much of her care to a nurse he was forced to employ when he became physically unable to handle the arduous tasks required of him. When Evelyn was eventually moved to a nursing home, she graciously accepted what was best for her. But Fred didn't!

Evelyn had a devout faith in God that sustained her; Fred did not. She was prepared to die long before her actual death.

Her faith was strong and her love for Christ never wavered. She did not fear death and actually looked forward to the transition from the pain she was enduring in this life to the next life where there would be no more pain. Her heart was filled with praise and joy as she looked toward Heaven.

When Evelyn's life on earth ended, Fred could not and, would not, accept the reality of her death. For days and days he wandered around barely aware of where he was or what he was doing. He continued to talk to her as if she were still alive. He shed no tears and displayed no other outward sign of emotion at her loss. Eventually, he came to recognize that she was gone; however, to this day, he still refuses to accept her death. He has become a bitter, angry recluse, preoccupied with his loss.

Fred has rejected the many attempts by his family, friends, minister, and others to provide him support. He has also refused professional counseling for his behavior. *Is he mentally ill?* No, not now. *Will he become mentally ill?* Very probably—most likely! *Is he physically ill?* Yes, definitely! *What is the cause of this illness?* There is no doubt that the unresolved guilt that he is carrying is largely responsible.

Almost everything in life can be either good or bad. This is also true of grief. Grief, depending on how we deal with it, can either be a healing process that cleanses and restores or it can, as in Fred's case, harm and destroy. God has blessed us with marvelous recuperative powers. We must trust in Him and allow ourselves to work through our grief. He will provide whatever strength we may lack. All we have to do is look to Him. This is the natural and healthy way to deal with grief.

Generally, grief is less severe if a person has lost a loved one to a lingering illness. This is because when death is anticipated, they have had an opportunity to work through and deal with many of the issues. However, only the one who is experiencing the grief fully understands the severity of what they are experiencing. Grief belongs to the individual experiencing it—the grieving person must carry the burden in his own way. We can comfort; we can console; we can "be there" when needed; but we cannot share the grief of another.

The path through grief generally follows a pattern that may include: shock, denial, anger, depression, and guilt before going on to acceptance. These terms are the ones that best describe the process I followed in dealing with my own grief and are consistent with terms used by other writers. How one grieves will depend upon his or her ability to cope with stress, deal with emotions, knowledge of and familiarity with the process of death and dying, relationship to the deceased, circumstances of death, support received, religious beliefs, and other factors.

For everyone who loses a loved one to death, shock will definitely be a factor. Shock, because we do not want to face or accept the reality of our loss, serves as an anesthetic that cushions us against the blow. We may feel numb and totally removed from what is happening, as if we are living in a dream. We may not be totally rational in our thinking and speech. Our stomach may feel as though it is tied in knots and feelings of severe weakness may overwhelm us. The degree of shock experienced normally will vary with the cause of death. For example, if the loss is sudden or unanticipated— an accident or sudden heart attack—the shock can, and often will be, severe, lasting days, weeks, months and, in extreme cases, even years. When the death is anticipated, the shock will normally be less severe and, in most cases, rather short-lived.

When we lost Don, Elsie and I were unable to view his body. As a result, there was no closure. The thought always remained with us that perhaps he wasn't really killed in the accident. As we looked down on the closed casket, it was heartbreaking not to be able to see him. *Was it really Don in that casket?* Occasionally, I still ask myself that same question. Denial is common and can be expected when a loved one has died.

We are most likely to refer to the death of one we love with such statements as: "he is gone, she passed away," or "we lost her," and to avoid terms like "death, died," or "dead" that imply finality. To this day, it is sometimes difficult for me to say that my sons are dead or have died; instead, I find myself substituting "passed away" or "we have lost."

For some time after the death of each of our boys, I would startle myself with such thoughts as, *I must show this to Dave*, or, *I must tell Don about this*. One time, shortly after John's death, Elsie and I were driving along a street in Pasco when I saw a young man who resembled John. My heart fluttered and nearly stopped. *Could he be . . . could he possibly be John?* Fighting for composure, I pulled over to the curb and stopped. "Elsie," I said, "there's a young man behind us walking this way who strongly resembles John." After turning the car around, we drove back toward the young man. As we drew near, Elsie became faint at heart as she, too, recognized the resemblance.

Denial can last in some form for months or even years. For example, the room in the house belonging to the deceased may be left unchanged and unoccupied for an indefinite period of time. Others may avoid visiting the grave.

Anger, as a phase of grief, is a normal response and needs to be expressed. Frequently, it is an indication that the healing process has begun. Anger may be demonstrated mildly, or in a blind rage—irrational and uncontrolled. No matter how it is expressed, it serves as an outlet for our pain, suffering, anguish, frustration, and feelings of helplessness.

Unresolved anger may lead to unresolved grief. Let the anger out! Screaming, crying, beating on a pillow and physical exercise are good releases for anger. At the very least, the bereaved should talk with someone about their feelings of anger. Many men and women can't bring themselves to show their true emotions to others, including anger. Quite often we say things to them like, "I admire your bravery," or "You're taking it well." Unfortunately, our well intentioned words do not bring comfort or alleviate their inner feelings. If our society would stop demanding that people refrain from doing what is normal and allow them to release their natural emotions, the grief experience would be far less difficult.

Being so very susceptible to guilt, man is able to turn almost any thought, feeling, experience or memory into guilt. This guilt may be real, unreal, or just the exaggeration of some small mistake. Feelings of guilt are nearly always inevitable when dealing with the death of a loved one. For quite some time after the death of each of our boys, I would have pangs of guilt if I laughed, enjoyed a television program, or even allowed my thoughts to dwell on something other than the death. Whether real or imagined, the consequences of any feeling of guilt is self-reproach—a self-reproach that must eventually be dealt with.

Guilt feelings must be communicated. Talking to a family member, friend, minister, doctor, or counselor generally relieves one of unrealistic guilt. For example, Elsie and I found that through revealing and sharing our feelings with each other and with others, we were able to lessen the oppression that comes from self-reproach. *Why didn't we insist that David not buy that motorcycle? Why did we allow Don to keep his car keys when we knew he didn't have a driver's license? Why did we allow Marilyn into our house that fateful day when John died?* These thoughts, and many more, coursed through our minds for a long time. Even today, after all this time, these feelings will still occasionally surface.

Real guilt, where one has actually contributed to the death of a loved one by deed or omission, is an entirely different matter and can be devastating. It can lead to alcoholism, abuse of legal and illegal drugs, physical or mental illness, even suicide.

Frank Wilson insisted that his wife accompany him to a basketball game even though, because of severe weather conditions, she was reluctant to go. On the way home, Frank lost control of his car due to slippery road conditions and slid into the path of an oncoming van. The head-on crash killed his wife instantly. Frank is living with unresolved guilt. His health is deteriorating rapidly.

Sandy Perkins whose teenage daughter Nancy slashed her wrists to end her life did so because of apparent hopelessness and helplessness. The suicide note she left behind revealed that she was involved in an irreconcilable love affair with a married man—her high school counselor. After her death, Sandy recalled several instances where her daughter had tried to "reach out" to her; however, she was so involved with her work and personal life that she failed to recognize the attempts. The symptoms were there, but she didn't recognize them and was too busy to see them. *If she had been there for her daughter, could she have made a difference?* A question that only she has to live with and only God can answer.

In my opinion, it is impossible for the loved ones of a person who has taken their life through suicide to escape feelings of guilt. Nearly every instance of suicide leaves at least one survivor with a complex of guilt. Generally, this guilt can be dealt with by talking with another family member, friend or a minister; however, those having deep-seated guilt should seek professional counseling.

Gerald Roberts and his family moved from St. Louis to Los Angeles when Gerald was given a promotion by the corporation where he was employed. His oldest son, Darrell, 15 at the time, was a model student and a well-behaved teenager. Some time after moving to L.A., Darrell became involved with drugs through his association with his newly-found friends. He was soon dealing drugs in order to feed his growing habit. One night he overdosed at a party and by the time his "stoned" friends realized that something was wrong, it was too late.

Because of his decision to move his family to Los Angeles, Gerald feels he is at fault. He has not been able to resolve his conflict with guilt.

Death comes as a result of man's original sin and; therefore, is an enemy of God and the last enemy of man. It was not God's intent that man should die. In I Corinthians 15:25-26, the Apostle Paul wrote, "For He must reign until He has put all His enemies under His feet." The last enemy to be destroyed is death.

Expressing our faith that the separation from our loved ones is, in reality, only a moment in time and that we will soon join them in eternal life, reduces the pain of their loss. Only their *bodies*, their earthly vessels, have died! Their *lives* continue on for all eternity in new and glorious spiritual bodies. Knowing that I will soon join my sons, makes Heaven much closer to me. I miss them! Oh, how I miss them! But to wish them back and take them away from the perfection of standing in God's presence would be selfish and unfair. I have no idea when God will call me home; however, until that day comes, I want to live my life in the best way possible—with happiness and love, as I strive to serve Christ and follow His will. Oh, I'm sure there will be hard times ahead, periods of recurring grief and moments of guilt. But not to worry, God will sustain! *Faith and hope are my strongest armor.*

The acceptance of our loss will lead to the reconstruction of our lives. We can recover from our sorrow. Faith is a poweful tool. We can experience growth. Growth in spirit and in mind! Growth in spiritual living! Growth beyond what we have ever known!

It's vitally important for a grieving person to return to the normal routine of life as soon as possible. Oh, it won't be the same—it will never be the same—but one can return to work, resume normal activities, and enjoy the pleasures that were, and must continue to be, a part of normal living.

When old sorrows return, and they will, they must be spoken of openly and honestly. Instead of grieving about "what might have been," build upon the memories of "what was." Elsie and I, in fond memory of our sons, make it a point to have the favorite food of each on the dates of their birth.

Reconstruction may include dramatic changes in life style. One may find that a move to a new location is necessary. If married, the surviving spouse, as they assume the responsibilities once accomplished by their deceased mate, will find that their role has changed and may resent it. This, in turn, can bring on feelings of guilt. Some, for financial reasons, may find it necessary to obtain a job for the first time or return to work after being away from the work force for many years. These people may have a great deal of difficulty making the transition. Indeed, others may find it necessary to enter college or a trade school to prepare themselves to earn a livelihood. This is never easy.

Reconstruction is well illustrated by the following story: Terry and Teresa Hanson were glowing with happiness. They were married only two days earlier and were enjoying their honeymoon. Life was pure ecstasy. *What more could Teresa want?* She had a loving husband whom she had known for more than two years who came from a fine family. Just a year before, Terry had received his doctorate in Marine Biology and was now employed as an assistant professor by a major university near San Diego. To marry, Teresa had left Oklahoma City and a promising career in finance. *Oh well, maybe she would resume her career at a later time.*

It was a gorgeous day on the island of Oahu. The skies were blue and a soft breeze stirred the air on a balmy afternoon. Terry and Teresa were driving along the ocean shore enjoying the tropical breeze, the resplendent beauty of the land, and the magnificence of the blue Pacific. Suddenly Terry exclaimed, "Look Honey, over there. That looks like a great place to surf!" He was pointing toward the water off a small beach.

"But," Teresa asked with apprehension, "do you think you can handle that surf?"

When he exclaimed, with a twinkle in his eye and an infectious grin, "Honey, you know I'm the best!" Teresa couldn't help but smile back and put her apprehensions on the back burner.

As he removed his surfboard from the roof of their rented car, he asked, "Want to try it? I'll get your surfboard down, too!"

Teresa, looking at the size of the waves and fully realizing her limited skills at surfing, declined. "No, that's okay, you go ahead." After kissing his bride, he picked up the board and ran off toward the clear, blue water.

"Are you certain it's safe to surf here, sweetheart?" Teresa called out as he swam out to catch a wave. "No one else is surfing and you aren't familiar with these waters."

Perhaps he didn't hear her. In any event, he didn't answer. She continued to watch as, minutes later, after catching a "big one," he skillfully rode his board shoreward. *And then she saw it!* Terror engulfed her as a rolling wave revealed a huge jagged rock directly ahead of her husband. She screamed and waved her arms trying to get his attention; however, the crashing surf hitting the beach was so loud he didn't hear her and remained totally unaware of the danger.

She watched in horror, helpless, as his surfboard hit the rock, throwing him high in the air. He landed in the water head first. Anxiously, she waited for him to surface—in vain! Only his surfboard was visible momentarily bobbing on the crest of a wave.

Frantically, she ran to the highway to seek help. Screaming and waving her arms, she was able to halt a passing motorist. She quickly made known what had happened and the motorist roared away to seek help. Teresa, thinking only of her husband, rushed back to the car, hurriedly unfastened her surfboard, and then ran as fast as she could toward the ocean. She hit the water at full stride, slammed the surfboard down, and, with all the power she could muster, began swimming. Soon she was in the area of the rock, but, could not locate Terry. She continued to search in frenzied desperation, but to no avail. Within a few minutes, a U. S. Coast Guard Cutter arrived.

Teresa was hysterical. She was led away to a waiting ambulance to be sedated. Then, barely conscious from the effects of the shock and sedation, she was taken by ambulance to a nearby hospital.

The Coast Guard continued to look for Terry's body but were unsuccessful. His body washed ashore two days later.

Teresa's dreams were shattered. *Why,* she thought, *did this happen to me? Is God punishing me for something? Why did Terry have to die instead of me?* "Oh, God," she cried aloud, "Please let me die!" She seriously thought of suicide as an option to escape from her pain. Her grief experience required professional care, both physical and psychological.

I must let go, she told herself, *Terry's gone! He's dead and, no matter what I do, I can't bring him back. The short time we had together was beautiful. The memories we shared can never be taken away from me and I will cherish them forever. No matter what happens, I will always remember Terry as he was: tall, handsome, muscular, a man of wisdom and a man of love. Life must go on! I have to be strong and, building upon what I have, move ahead.*

In realistically accepting her loss and with the support of a loving, caring family, Teresa began the reconstruction of her life. Eventually, she was able to return to Oklahoma City and the career she had left. When she resumed her church activities, her friends encouraged her to participate in social functions. At first she was reluctant, but soon found that she could laugh and have fun without feeling guilty about it. Over time, as she came to realize that she had much to look forward to in life, her attitude changed for the better. She discovered that, once again, happiness could find a place in her life. True, life without Terry would never be the same and there would always be a place for him in her heart; however, many of the pleasures of life she had once known were revived to be enjoyed again. No doubt, she will eventually find love and romance with another that will lead to the joy and happiness that only a family can bring.

Even though we carry our grief alone and no one can really share in it, we still urgently need the support of others. Our resilience will largely depend upon the amount, reaction to, and acceptance of the support we receive. Usually the greatest support comes from other family members with whom we share the common bond of love and grief. Such support, though generally highly emotional, is exceedingly strong because of these bonds. This close relationship can be conflicting because of the burden of grief experienced by each family member. For example, when a couple loses a child to death, each of them may be so overcome by his or her own grief that they are emotionally unable to provide any support for the other. Friends are able to lend support that family members are unable to give. Basic needs can be met and services provided. To know friends are there for them is a comfort to the bereaved. Spiritual leaders lend comfort as they come to the grieving with an open heart and mind, providing both communion and guidance as the burden of loss is placed before the throne of grace.

Support groups can be helpful for those sharing a common bond from similar experiences of loss. *Compassionate Friends,* and *Survivors of Suicide* are two such groups. There are many other groups that provide for the specific individual needs of men, women, or children as they deal with their loss.

Looking back, I think of many things that did and did not help during my own bereavement. Perhaps the most good is accomplished not by saying or doing, but by simply "being there." Just your very presence can often supply the help and support that is needed. One should be discreet in providing words of comfort and refrain from saying , "don't grieve, just stay busy, this, too, shall pass," or "be brave!" This only reflects your limited knowledge of the grieving process. Just the touch of a hand can mean so much more than empty words, no matter how sincere those words may be.

Offer your prayers, but do not force them. Remember, many people blame God for their loss and are angry with Him. For quite some time after the death, they may not want to have anything to do with God, prayers, church, or religion. Respect their feelings! If they ask about such things and you know the answers, answer. If not, arrange for a pastor or some other qualified person to contact them. Be warm and kind, accept tears, and cry with the bereaved if you feel so inclined. Be faithful to any commitments or promises you make. Be a good listener! Allow them to freely express their emotions and talk about their loss. Don't assume that you have to say a great deal—you don't! Just *be there*!!!

A pet can also be a source of strength and comfort for someone who has suffered a loss. JoJo has provided an abundance of comfort to both Elsie and me. He sensed our grief and was there to cuddle, hold, and listen to our words of sorrow. His presence supplied a kind of solace that cannot be brought by a person—only by a pet. Even though JoJo didn't understand our words, he understood our sorrow.

All of these sources can provide strength and comfort; however, the greatest source comes from the Lord Jesus Christ. Place your burden on Him. When you seek Him, He will draw nigh unto you and meet your every need. In Second Corinthians 12:9, He tells us, "My grace is sufficient for you; for My strength is made in weakness."

It may sound macabre, but I believe that every person, young and old, should prepare for death. Parents should discuss death with their children as soon as they are old enough to understand. As we teach our children about the facts of life, we should also teach them about the facts of death. Not only about the eventuality of their own death, but also of someone near and dear to them. This is not to imply or suggest that parents should dwell on death with their children; merely allow them to understand that death is a natural function of life. If children learn about death in this manner, when someone they love dies, the death experience will not be so uncomfortable. Acceptance becomes easier.

No doubt, the reason most people fail to ponder their own mortality is because of their fear of death. This need not be. No one, with the possible exception of those in intense pain or suffering, looks forward to dying. We fear the unknown! But there is no need to fear death! Indeed, we must face this, our last enemy, squarely. And, if we are fully prepared, we can do so with courage and faith.

From a materialistic standpoint, we should get our worldly affairs in order. If a will, trust and a *living will* have not been made, then one should see that these are taken care of. This can reduce the legal red tape and turmoil for loved ones.

Also, we should plan our own funeral. By doing so, we can ease the pain of our loved ones and avoid having them make hasty, and sometimes costly, decisions at a time when, emotionally, they are most vulnerable. It is truly a gift to our survivors. Others may tell of your virtues, choosing to ignore the fact that you had shortcomings, while you can plan your service to reflect your love for the Lord and your assurance of eternal life. This can provide great comfort to your family and friends; it is an act of love. Request that your favorite hymns and Scripture passages be used in the actual service.

Above all else, faith releases us from our fear of death, preparing us to face death and move through the transition to the glories of Heaven. With every passing day, I draw nearer to that time when, either through death or the rapture, I will meet Christ face-to-face and see the fullness of His glory. God has made Himself abundantly real to all mankind, and yet, there are those who fail to recognize His wondrous works.

CHAPTER SIX

Siblings Struggling With Grief

Mourning is a natural process, something that every person must go through in his or her own way; however, by fully understanding all the stages of grief, the hurting can be considerably lessened. It is a natural process that eventually leads to acceptance. In a healthy grief process, the survivors discover that, in spite of their loss, they have a right to live full and fruitful lives.

Though I've mentioned the subject previously, men are hampered in expressing emotion by masculine taboos. How great it would be if men would be more like women in expressing their emotions. Most women cry easily, which is good, while most men do not. Crying is intensely therapeutic, and generally will provide a more rapid recovery from any trauma. Our society is largely to blame. Little boys are told, "Quit your crying! Big boys don't cry!" They then carry this mentality and philosophy over into manhood, holding back their tears because they consider them to be a sign of weakness. *They are so very wrong*!

Women are also more inclined to turn to their female friends in intimate confidence, which is good, while men are less inclined to relate their intimate feelings to others. Once again, they are robbing themselves of a more rapid recovery. Verbally confiding one's intimate feelings with another, can, and most often will, provide an outlet that is necessary for recovery. Men who are unable to verbalize their feelings are more apt to express themselves physically or by verbal explosion.

We should encourage men and little boys to be more like women in this regard. What is wrong with crying? What is wrong with intimately discussing a problem with a family member or close friend? *Not a thing! It's something that should, and must, be done!* Failure to do these things is one of the basic reasons why men do not live as long as women. Every person—young or old—needs someone they can talk to and confide in.

All individuals haves to work through their grief in the way that is best for them. There are no easy answers or steps to follow. In researching material for this book, I was impressed with the fact that experts believe that we must allow grief to do its work; we must wade through the sorrowful grieving process; we must drink of the bitter cup. The reminders of our loved ones give us daily pain: the clothes, the books, the pictures, the letters, the empty place at the dinner table— the list is endless. And yet, in spite of being brokenhearted because of our feelings of loss, most of us would not want to be without these reminders. With the passage of time, they cause less pain and bring more joy. And what would we have without them? They are our tie to the past—our tie to loved ones who have gone home to be with the Lord!

Although most of us are concerned about our physical and emotional health, we entertain many misconceptions. It is essential that we encourage one another to grieve and to use the tear glands that the Lord gave us. Many people believe that tears show a lock of courage and faith when, in fact, they are a safety valve for the heart and body. Men often cry on the inside but never allow their tears to be seen outwardly. Some feel that shedding tears would be a reflection on their manhood and that they would be an embarrassment to themselves and others. How unfortunate that people can't understand the simple truth! It says in the Old Testament that stout-hearted men "lifted up their voice, and wept." (Job 1-12) David wept over the death of Saul. (II Samuel 1:12) and King Jehoash wept as the prophet Elisha's death approached (II Kings 13,14) David, the psalmist said, "My tears have been my food day and night." (Psalm 42:23)

In trying to "keep up appearances" without an emotional outlet we may be inflicting great physical harm on ourselves. It is a known fact that many phsyically ill patients are ill because of some unresolved situation involving stress and/or grief. Our physical health is closely connected to our emotional health and well-being.

These observations remind me of a young man who was killed in an automobile accident several years ago. Brandon Kennedy and his brother, Carl, were partners in an auto repair business. They had been close companions through childhood and high school, where they were star athletes, and were now enjoying a relationship as business partners. They not only worked together, they socialized together. Carl, married for six years, and his wife, Marie, were the parents of two little girls who not only were a delight to their parents, but also to their Uncle Brandon and grandparents, Joe and Mary Kennedy. Brandon, a year older than Carl, never married.

One evening, as they were closing up the shop for the day, Carl asked Brandon if he would mind driving their pickup truck to a neighboring town to pick up some auto parts they needed. Brandon, having a dinner date with a really cute "chick" he had recently met, declined, and asked Carl if he would go instead. Carl agreed and, after consuming a hurried dinner, left on the seventy mile trip.

Both Carl and Brandon were Christians as were their parents and Marie. They always made it a point to put God first in their lives. Marie, although she would never admit it, was jealous of all the time her husband spent with his brother. Inwardly, she resented their close relationship.

As Carl drove along a rather lonely stretch of road—a short cut he had taken to reduce traveling time—he thought of the family picnic and water skiing that had been planned for the coming Saturday. He was looking forward to being with his parents, brother, and the rest of his family.

Back in town, Brandon, as he hurried to close the shop for the day, suddenly remembered that the seat belt on the driver's side of the pickup was broken. He had planned on fixing it earlier in the day but, when the shop got busy, he completely forgot about it. He called Carl's home in an effort to catch him before he left but, he was already gone. *Oh well,* he told himself, *Carl's a careful driver, so there's really nothing to worry about.* But he couldn't get it off his mind.

It was shortly after 7:00 p.m. on an overcast day, and the sun had nearly set. Visibility was so limited that Carl turned on the headlights. Suddenly, about 300 yards ahead, he saw a car coming toward him at a high rate of speed, erratically weaving back and forth across the center line. In an effort to get out of the way, he pulled over onto the shoulder of the road and stopped. It didn't help! In horror he watched the car cross over the line and head directly toward him. The force of the impact rendered him unconscious. It also pushed the pickup off the road, over a bank, and into a creek bed more than 30 feet below. Carl was thrown free from the wreckage. The car, after landing on top of the truck, bounced off, and rolled over Carl.

Another motorist, traveling a short distance behind Carl, witnessed the accident and stopped to see what he could do to help. After quickly assessing the scene, he told his wife to drive to a nearby service station and call 911. Within minutes, two police cars arrived. The officers rushed to join the good Samaritan who was kneeling beside Carl. Miraculously, in spite of his pain and injuries, Carl was able to provide them with a brief account of what had happened. The driver of the other car kept mumbling, over and over, that he had to move his car. He was dazed, but not seriously injured, and so intoxicated his speech was almost incoherent. And, he was only seventeen!

When the ambulances arrived, the medics administered emergency treatment; then, after gingerly placing Carl on a stretcher and carrying him to one of the ambulances, rushed off to the nearest hospital, some 20 miles away. The other ambulance followed with the drunken seventeen year old.

Brandon and Marie arrived at the hospital simultaneously. Brandon's parents arrived shortly thereafter. A neighbor—a friend of Marie's—was staying with the girls. Brandon tried to talk to Marie,but she brushed him aside and turned her back. He was at a loss as to why she refused to acknowledge him. Both were told that Carl had been rushed to surgery and they would be informed of his progress. When the boys' parents entered the waiting room, they were brushed aside by Marie as they attempted to embrace her. They, too, were at a loss as to the cause of her strange behavior.

Eventually, a doctor, still dressed in green surgical clothing, entered the waiting area and asked Marie if she was the wife of Carl Kennedy. When Marie acknowledged that she was, he sat down beside her and introduced himself as Dr. Olsen. "Mrs. Kennedy," he began, "your husband sustained severe extensive internal injuries in the accident. His condition is critical and, if he is to have any chance of recovery, we must operate immediately. They've already taken him to the operating room. We won't know just how extensive his injuries are until after the operation. I'll be back to talk to you later."

As soon as the doctor departed, Joe, Carl's father, bowed his head and began to pray aloud that God would intercede on his son's behalf.

Two hours of waiting with baited breath brought no answer. *How long would it take before they knew?* Marie and Mary cried softly. Joe paced the floor with bowed head, occasionally brushing a tear from his eye. Brandon, somber, sat motionless, staring out the window at nothing, lost in his thoughts. *If only I had gone after the parts, none of this would have happened! It's all my fault that Carl's here! Where is that doctor anyway? Surely they should know something by now!*

As if in answer to Brandon's thoughts, Dr. Olsen entered the waiting room. Everyone looked to him in anticipation. Marie, jumping to her feet, asked, "How is he?"

The pained expression on the doctor's face revealed the answer. "I'm very sorry!" he said, placing a comforting hand on Marie's shoulder. "We did everything we could, but . . . his injuries were too severe . . ."

Joe, seeing that Mary was near collapse, placed his arms around her and held her close. They clung together in mutual support. At first, Brandon's mind refused to accept the doctor's words. However, when the reality of Carl's death finally registered, his face turned ashen and he was overcome by an unbelievable, heavy-burden of guilt.

"No! It isn't true!" Marie screamed. "It can't be! You must be mistaken!"

"It's true, Mrs. Kennedy. I'm sorry!" Dr. Olsen said as he turned to leave. "If there's anything I can do . . . "

Livid with rage, Marie lunged toward where Brandon was sitting by the window. "It's all your fault," she screamed, wildly swinging her arms. "You killed him! You're the one who should be dead—not Carl!"

Joe, with assistance from Dr. Olsen, was able to restrain Marie from assaulting Brandon; however, she remained inconsolable in her grief and anger. At that moment, Marie's mother, whom she had called earlier, arrived and led her out of the waiting room to the corridor. Soon the mother returned to the waiting room, apologized to all and departed for home with Marie.

Joe, overwrought with grief and emotion, asked Brandon if he would drive them home. It was a quiet trip. His parents were oblivious of everything around them and Brandon, as he drove, said not a word and gave no outward expression of the emotion that he was feeling. His inward struggle with himself was becoming unbearable.

The next morning, Brandon reluctantly picked up the morning paper knowing that it would contain an account of Carl's fatal crash. And, it did! There it was in bold head-lines! At first, not able to face the pain, he set the paper aside; then, picking it back up, forced himself to read it. "Oh, my God, no!" he exclaimed, as he read a quotation by the officer who investigated the accident: "The victim would probably have survived the accident had he been wearing a seat belt and shoulder restraint."

Oh, God, he thought, as his pounding fists tore through the kitchen wall. *What have I done? Marie was right! It was my fault! I am to blame*! Filled with guilt and hatred toward himself, he still shed no tears. These feelings intensified when, a few minutes later, the phone rang. The woman on the line was screaming so loudly that, at first, her words were totally incoherent. He recognized Marie's voice and, by listening closely, finally was able to make out what she was saying. "You murderer! You killer! I hate you! I hate you!" She repeated it over and over several times before slamming down the receiver.

With Carl's death, Brandon's entire life changed. The old enthusiasm and zest for life were gone. Now, he was a beaten, bitter man without purpose. Marie's refusal to allow him to see his nieces added to his depression. He knew that they, too, would be upset and depressed by their mother's decision not to allow them to see their "favorite uncle."

Six months went by with Brandon attempting to bypass the grief process. During this time he became a mental and physical wreck and his business fell to an all-time low. Of course, he had no way of knowing that one-fourth of all hospital patients are in the hospital because of unresolved grief. And, even if he had known, he was in no state of mind to realize that if he didn't change, it could also happen to him.

Slowly, with the help of his parents and pastor, he started to put the pieces of his life back together. This process started the day he was at his parent's home. They were all sitting around the kitchen table sharing with one another the joyous times they used to have with Carl and the things they had done together. When his dad shared a tender moment about Carl and his little girls, tears came to Brandon's eyes. The first tears he had shed since Carl's death.

His mom, noticing the tears, said, "Let it go, Son. Open your heart to God! Tears are God's safety valve for the heart!"

What at first were only a few tears became, within moments, a flow of wetness running down his cheeks. With the tears came the Holy Spirit. An hour later, when the tears stopped, he found that the heavy burden of guilt he had been carrying was gone. His spirit was lifted.

A few days later, his spirit soared again when he answered a knock on his door. It was Marie and the girls! "Oh, Brandon," she said, her eyes brimming with tears, "can you ever find it in your heart to forgive me for the way I've been treating you?"

Words weren't necessary. He opened his arms and welcomed her with a warm embrace. Within seconds the girls, too, were affectionately clinging to him. It felt good!

After going inside, Marie continued. "I'm so ashamed of the way I've acted. It's just that I've been so insanely jealous and envious of you that I allowed it to cloud my mind and heart with hate. It took a psychoanalyst to open my eyes . . . and God to open my heart."

"It's okay! I'm just glad that you and the kids are back in my heart . . . and in my life!"

Marie, since Carl's death, has become every active in the

87

MADD organization (**M**others **A**gainst **D**runk **D**rivers) and speaks to many women's groups and other organizations.

Often, when a child dies, the remaining children don't know how to handle the death or how to deal with what they are feeling. A child often does not understand death. They need a great deal of comfort and attention during this time. It's only logical that they turn to their parents for these needs and for answers to their many questions. It is unfortunate that many times, because of their own grief, the parents, are not emotionally available to them.

A child must be told the truth about death. Far too many adults, especially when the child is only four or five, wrongly assume that the child is too young to be told. They may have the best of intentions when they say that the dead person is "sleeping," and believe that they are shielding the child from the true significance of death and the burden of reality. The child can clearly see through such denial. Remember, as a member of the family, they deserve and have the right to know the truth. There are children who have been scarred for life because they were not counseled and prepared properly regarding the reality of death.

Many children learn the following bedtime prayer and recite it nightly, never knowing the meaning of what they are saying or the concept of dying:

> Now I lay me down to sleep,
> I pray the Lord my soul to keep.
> If I should die before I wake,
> I pray the Lord my soul to take.

Parents should not wait until a death in the family before discussing death and dying with their children. The subject should be dealt with honestly in conjunction with birth, the body and the soul. A child needs to know that the body is only a shell and human life is lived within that shell. When the body dies, life continues but the body decays as will all vegetable and animal matter that dies. Because of the emotional impact, it may be too difficult immediately after the death of a child for parents to talk to the other children. Generally, a warm hug and a kiss will suffice until emotional control is reestablished. However, a full explanation of the death should be given as soon as possible.

Should a young child attend the funeral of a deceased sibling? This is a question that parents should discuss with one another and the child. If the child is old enough to understand death, they should be given the option of deciding if they want to attend or not. Viewing the body, or perhaps even touching the deceased in a gesture of good-bye, may greatly relieve the questioning mind of the child. Certainly the experience of going to the funeral home provides the child with a better understanding of death and the death process.

The surviving children must be prepared for the changes in day-to-day living. The entire household will be affected. There will be a missing place at the table. If the survivor is a sibling, perhaps there will be no one to play with after school; no one to argue with and, *yes*, no one to fight with. And, perhaps the most difficult change—no one in the adjacent bed. Some of these changes may require examination by the parents and discussion with the children. In some cases, the household may require some minor, or perhaps even major, alteration.

Parents should carefully observe their surviving children on a daily basis for a period of time after the death to ensure that the child is not in denial. Denial hinders the grief process and healing from the loss. Some denial is normal and is soon resolved; however, if it is acute and lasts for any length of time the children or child may require more in-depth counseling with a professional who has had training and experience in dealing with death and dying. Allowing the child to attend a child support group may also be beneficial. Sometimes the child may experience a deep depression or suffer severe feelings of worthlessness. Parents should be alert to these things and, if found, seek help immediately.

Parents, when frustrated because of the loss of their child, may be inclined to vent that frustration on their surviving children. Careful monitoring of themselves and one another may help identify and control such behavior. It is also not uncommon for parents who have lost a child to place the memory of that child up on a pedestal. This is not healthy for them or their surviving children. Constantly extolling the dead child's virtues and minimizing their faults may cause deviate behavior in, and be harmful to, the other children.

A child, after the death of a sibling, may suffer what is called "Survivors Guilt Syndrome." No matter how irrational it may seem, they blame themselves for the death. They may ask themselves, "Why him or her and not me?" They may even recall how, in a moment of anger, they said, "I wish you were dead!" not realizing that those words might be the last their brother or sister would ever hear them say. Or perhaps they thought something along that line but didn't say it. This, too, can cause a severe episode of Survivors Guilt Syndrome.

A little more than two years after John's death, Michael and I were driving from Redmond to Bend in central Oregon. We were discussing the deaths of his brothers. "Dad," he said, "I've gone through their deaths over and over again in my mind. The death of one brother would be difficult, but when multiplied by three . . . it's been nearly unbearable. Especially John's death. It was so senseless—so meaningless. Bill and I were devastated by his death; but, it must have been pure torture for you and Mom. Dad, how could he do such a thing when he had so much to live for?" Without waiting for an answer, he continued, "I've been so angry with him for putting us through this torment and torture. But, Dad, I love him so! I miss him so! Oh, God, how I miss him!"

For a few moments, not knowing what to say, I sat in silence. *How I loved this son of mine.* I was so proud of him and his accomplishments. A true scholar, he had completed

90

his B.S. degree at Sacramento State University, while married to Darrellyne. With a degree in Pharmacy he first worked in Redmond, Oregon and then continued his practice in Vancouver, Washingtron. As the divorced father of two children, Sheila and Eric, I knew he was thinking of his love for them when he spoke of my losses and feelings.

Speaking in a shaky voice, I looked at him and said what I knew to be true, "Son, I miss them, too, but just think what a joyous reunion it will be when we meet them on those golden shores of Heaven!" We continued on in silence, each lost in our own thoughts. Warm tears seeped through my lashes and dropped softly to my cheeks. The words from I John 2:10 "He that loveth his brother abideth in the light . . . " came to mind.

CHAPTER SEVEN

The Bereaved Parent

Nearly a quarter of a century after Ricky's death, Bill and I were lounging in his back yard. We had been discussing his Vietnam experiences and the problem of having to be away from home a great deal while serving as a warrant officer in the U. S. Army. "It was really difficult," he said, "especially when Ricky was killed." Although we had shared the story many times, it was obvious that he had a need to talk about it again.

"Here I was in Vietnam, thousands of miles from home, relaxing between missions, partying with some of the other guys in my remote unit in the Delta when a pilot friend came to tell me that there was an emergency in my family and I was to go to Saigon immediately."

"That must have really upset you!"

"It did, especially when he had no idea what the emergency was. Anyway, they made arrangements for me to fly to Saigon on a fighter plane. A command representative met me there and told me that Ricky had been critically injured. That's all he knew, he didn't have any of the details. Finally, the required paperwork for my emergency leave was completed and I was placed on the next flight to the States. It was the longest flight of my life. For the next eighteen hours I didn't sleep a wink, just sat there staring into space worrying and wondering what had happened."

"When and how did you find out?"

"As soon as we landed in San Francisco, with my heart pounding, I ran to the nearest pay phone and called Pam. My heart stood still as she told me that our little boy had died. Dad," he continued, "after I heard how severely injured he was, I was almost relieved that he didn't survive. I took solace in knowing that his few years on earth had been happy ones. My only regret was the small amount of time I had with him—I was overseas the day he was born and overseas the day that he died."

"But, Bill, you couldn't help it, the Army . . . "

"I know, but the guilt tore away at my insides. Intensive psychoanalysis, along with treatment for alcoholism and post-traumatic stress disorder, helped me deal with it. Now I don't feel the guilt, only the loss—a loss I've learned to bear."

"I know what you mean, it's something I've had to do, too."

He continued on. "Where once there were three children, now there was only two—Angie and Brian. Those two did wonders in helping to fill the void in my heart and making me realize that life must go on. I finally came to accept Ricky's death. You know, Dad, I've only visited his grave twice . . . and have no intention of ever returning. Ricky's not there—only a grave containing his earthly remains."

"Bill, I agree with you; he's not there. However, in fond memory of your brothers, your mom and I still continue to visit their graves. Somehow, going to the cemetery helps us feel closer to them—and to God. Usually we take flowers for their graves and spend some time in prayer thanking God for the years that we had them with us. I think you should visit Ricky's grave. When we fail to visit the gravesite of a loved one, we diminish them in our minds. Son, I fully understand how memories can swell our hearts with pain, making it easier not to go; but, we should go anyway because it's part of the loving process."

To illustrate, I told him about the short life of little Bobby Jones. Bobby was a typical eight year old—full of energy, handsome, and very bright—a true delight to his parents. All through the summer vacation from school he was fine; however, soon after school opened in the fall, he became listless and lost his appetite. Concerned, his parents took him to their pediatrician. After a thorough examination and some lab work, the doctor informed them that Bobby had leukemia. Understandably, they were upset and alarmed. However, when the doctor told them that the prognosis was encouraging and that, with treatment, he could and probably would recover, it helped relieve their anxiety.

When they sat down with Bobby to tell him what was wrong, he seemed to understand and accept it much better than they had ever dreamed he would. They were confident he would get better. And, he did . . . for a while. Then, several months later, he took a turn for the worse and was confined to a hospital bed.

Bobby's family had a deep, abiding faith in God and faithfully attended church. Many prayers were lifted up on Bobby's behalf. Even though his condition continued to worsen, his parents would not give up and continued to tell themselves that he would get well. They talked with him about all the things they would do together when he got better and returned home. They made short and long range plans for him and encouraged him to look toward a bright, long, and eventful life.

One evening when he seemed to be at his lowest, Bobby looked up at his parents, smiled, and said, "I want to go home."

Taking his hand in hers, his mom reassuringly said, "I know you do. Maybe some day soon . . . "

"No, Mom," he said, interrupting her, "I want to go to Heaven."

His mom and dad looked at each other in amazement. Bobby knew he was going to die soon and was now ready to go to his heavenly home.

Even though Bobby was aware of his impending death and had come to accept it, his parents had not. It was more difficult for them to accept. They knew, however, that they had to gain control of themselves and their emotions so they could be strong for Bobby. His pain and discomfort had increased and the end was near. To encourage him, they read from the Bible and talked to him about Heaven and the joys that were soon to be his.

A few nights later they were standing beside his bed looking down at the emaciated body of their son writhing in pain. Suddenly, he stopped moving around, opened his eyes, and looked up at them. He smiled and a warm glow of peace lit up his little face as his life slipped from his body to begin the journey to his heavenly home.

Another story that gives me a great deal of satisfaction and confirms my belief in how close we are to Heaven, is that of little five year old Cynthia who lay dying in the hospital— the victim of a drunken driver in a crash that had claimed the life of her mother and baby sister.

In the late afternoon of the previous day, Nancy, her mother, took her two little girls with her to pick up Frank, their father, from his place of work at a sheet metal plant some eight to ten miles from their home. Nancy was driving at a moderate speed, carefully observing her surroundings. There was a small hill on her left that blocked the view of any traffic that might enter or cross the highway at an upcoming crossroad; however, she knew that she had the right of way and that any traffic coming off the crossroad had to stop. Suddenly, right at the crossroads, she saw a car traveling at a high rate of speed coming directly at her from the left. It was obvious that the driver could not stop in time. In a blink of an eye it was over. According to witnesses, the crash was devastating, almost totally destroying both vehicles. Nancy and her youngest daughter were pronounced dead on arrival at the hospital, while Cynthia, in a coma, barely clung to life. As so often is the case, the drunken driver sustained only minor injuries.

Frank, looking down upon the only living member of his family, allowed a prayer to pour from his heart to his lips. A nurse was constantly by her side monitoring every breath and heartbeat. Earlier the doctor had told him that her life could slip away at any moment. Suddenly Cynthia opened her eyes. Her lips parted, forming a radiant smile. Her face seemed to glow. Then, in a faint, soft little voice, she said, "Grandpa! I'm coming, Grandpa! Wait for me!" Closing her eyes, she breathed her last breath.

Frank's heart was broken as he watched the last bit of life ebb from his darling daughter. His mind was filled with confusion. *Who*, he thought, *was she talking to? Her grandfathers were both living and in reasonably good health.* Only minutes later, his unspoken question was answered when he learned that Cynthia's maternal grandfather had suffered a fatal heart attack and died about an hour earlier. Somehow, God, in his love and mercy, had given her a glimpse of her beloved grandpa and Heaven.

Needless to say, Frank is living with a fractured heart. But life must go on. He is determined to find a semblance of reason for what has happened and to live his life for God in honor of his beloved family.

We sat silently for a few minutes, my thoughts dwelling upon Bill and where life had brought him. He had a very successful career in the military. After serving two tours in Vietnam, he was given the opportunity to attend the University of Tampa in Florida and graduated magna cum laude with a degree in Criminology. He became fluent in Spanish as well as Vietnamese as a result of his assignments. After retirement he continued his education, receiving a M.A. degree in Social Work. God had richly blessed Bill and his family. He and his wife Pam continue to reside at Greenacres in the Spokane Valley. Their daughter Angie married and she and her husband Jeff are the proud parents of two children, Becca 7, and Matthew 5. Elsie and I are delighted to be great-grandparents. And their son Brian is 24, single, and works for a bank in Seattle.

My thoughts returned to the present. "Bill," I said, "we're very fortunate. Our marriages survived the tragedies that life brought into our lives. So many marriages are torn apart by grief and end in separation or divorce. When the grief is common, as with the death of a child, the stress can become so great that support for each other is at best, difficult, and sometimes, non-existent. We should thank God every day for being there for us and our wives."

With tears in my eyes, I ended our conversation by saying, "Son, your mom and I love you and Pam. You know that. we want the very best for you. Remember, God will bless you . . . allow Him to do so!"

CHAPTER EIGHT

To Live or Die: A Choice?

He was twenty-eight. John had enjoyed living with us in his little apartment on the lower floor of our home, and we enjoyed having him with us. He had his meals with his mother and me and spent a good deal of time socializing with us, but also had the privacy of his own apartment to entertain his friends. John was devoted to us, and we to him. He readily and willingly offered his services to a friend in need. There was an abundance of girlfriends in his life, and, although he had gone steady with two or three, each for a short period of time, he had never found the "right" one. As an employee, he applied himself and proved that he was loyal and trustworthy.

Yes, John loved life and people; he also loved Christ whom he had received into his heart. However, thus far, his life had been unfulfilled. He wasn't sure of what he wanted to do in life, or even what he was capable of doing. Mechanically inclined, he enjoyed working on, and operating, motorized equipment. We often discussed potential avenues of employment, some of which he pursued.

Whenever John was unsuccessful at doing something, he quickly became discouraged and despondent about what he saw as his failure. Although he had his periods of depression, he was generally happy and enjoyed life. He would readily express his feelings to his mom and me and regularly sought our advice and counseling.

It is now my belief that my son harbored thoughts of suicide for several days, perhaps weeks, before completing the act. I doubt if he had decided exactly "when," but am quite certain that he had probably considered "how." When he did die, I am not sure that it was intentional; perhaps he simply wanted to draw the attention of Marilyn. Without question, he was so desperate that it really didn't matter to him.

I'm sorry that I didn't have the knowledge about suicide then that I have now. If people would educate themselves and have a better understanding of the self-destruction process, many suicides could and would be prevented. The enigma of suicide still remains. *Why would one want to take his or her own life?* There are many reasons! Suicide is "completed" by people from all races and walks of life: from the very young to the very old, from the very poor to the very rich, from the lesser intelligent to the highly intelligent, from the very religious to the non-religious, by both men and women and boys and girls.

I use the term *completed* suicide rather than *committed* suicide because many researchers and suicidologists feel that the majority of suicides are not completed by choice. Their findings indicate that at least 70 percent of all suicides are associated with depression. Some researchers feel that nearly all suicides are so related. In other words, the suicidal person suffering from depression does not have a choice. He or she cannot reasonably look at the alternatives and consequences and make a choice. Those suffering from clinical depression have a suicide rate 25 times higher than the general population.

The suicidal person feels there is no other course of action available to them, everything is hopeless, and dying is the only way to resolve the pain and anguish they feel. If, however, they could make a rational choice, it would not be suicide. They don't necessarily want to die, but feel that there is no reason to continue living. Death may not be preferable, but life is intolerable.

A soldier who, in battle, sacrifices his life by throwing himself on a grenade to save the lives of his comrades is probably not doing so because of depression. Nor, perhaps, is the thrill seeker who goes beyond the bounds of reason in playing a game of Russian Roulette. And, of course, a suicide by impulse may be by choice. But who can be certain that, even in these cases, there might not be an underlying depression depriving the person of their ability to make a rational decision.

Recently, I read about two pre-teen boys who, just prior to jumping to their deaths from a high bridge, left a note saying that they were doing so because they wanted to see what life after death would be like. In another case, the TV news reported that a young girl had taken her life so she could continue to be with her dying mother.

There are many accidental, unintentional suicides, every year. For example, I recently read about a woman who, for attention, ingested a lethal dose of a prescription drug expecting her husband to find her when he returned from work at 4:30 p.m—something that she had done several times in the past. Unfortunately, her husband didn't come home at his usual time. He called around 5:30 to let her know that he was working late and wouldn't be there until 7:30, but there was no answer. When he did arrive, he found her lifeless body.

It has been estimated that at least 15 percent of all single occupant auto fatalities are suicides. This figure should probably be much, much, higher; however, many such deaths are recorded as accidental. When an accident occurs, no one knows for sure if it was truly an accident. *Did the driver accidentally cross over the center line and hit the oncoming car? Or, did they do so intentionally?*

Some people thrive living on the edge of destruction and flirting with death. They live and drive recklessly, placing their own lives and the lives of others in jeopardy. The number of lives taken each year by those driving drunk or those who are high on drugs is truly appalling. It is estimated that approximately 5 percent of all Americans are alcoholics and about 15 percent of them will die by their own hand. These alcohol related deaths account for 30 percent of the suicides in America. Many, if not most, of the deaths that occur each day as a result of alcohol or drug overdoses are actually indirect suicides.

Fifteen percent of acute anorexics will die as a result of their eating disorder. No doubt the percentage of deaths from acute bulimia, another eating disorder, is comparable. Such deaths could well be classified as indirect suicides. Overeating, too, especially by those who have been warned by their physicians that their continued eating habits could result in death, also could be placed in the indirect suicide category. An example of this is the famous Diamond Jim Brady who was told by his doctor that death was imminent if he continued to eat in the manner to which he was accustomed. He ignored the warning and died within months.

While researching for this book, I completed an in-depth study of suicide and was amazed at the statistics. Every year in the United States there are approximately 30,000 suicides— 12 for every 100,000 people. Or, to put it another way, every year between one and two percent of all Americans take their own lives. Overall, this makes suicide the eighth leading cause of death in this country; however, for young people between the ages of 10 and 24 it is the second leading cause of death.

Women attempt suicide three times more often than do men, but men complete the suicide four times more often than women. This, no doubt, can be partially explained because women, more so than men, use the attempt of suicide as a cry for help and as a means of manipulation. It can further be explained by the different methods for suicide chosen by the sexes. Women are more inclined to overdose on prescription drugs or slash their wrists, methods that are generally not as successful as those utilized by men who choose more lethal methods such as firearms, hanging or poison. In recent years; however, due to the trend of women purchasing and carrying firearms for safety and protection, the number of women choosing to use a firearm to end their lives is on the increase.

Although only one to two percent of Americans actually die from suicide, at least four to five percent attempt suicide at some point during their lifetime. And, of those who attempt suicide, ten percent will eventually succeed, two percent within a year. It is estimated that 25 to 40 percent of those who eventually complete the suicide have made a prior attempt.

Attitudes about suicide have varied, sometimes widely, throughout the history of man. Through eons of time, some have had attitudes that respected self-destruction as an honorable way to die. Government officials, rather than being forced to reveal vital information when captured, have placed lethal capsules of poison under their tongues. Another example is the Japanese kamikaze pilot who, by willingly flying his bomb-laden airplane into a U.S. warship and sacrificing his life, honored himself and his country. Others, as late as the last century, and even into this century, have looked upon self-destruction as being sinful, evil, a work of the devil. In some churches, it was forbidden to conduct a funeral service for a person who committed suicide or allow their body to be buried in the hallowed ground of a church cemetery. Such a death was considered murder and the victim was doomed to Hell. The survivors of a suicide victim were often ostracized and forced to endure unbelievable physical and mental anguish.

Thankfully, attitudes toward the victims of suicide and their survivors have changed for the better since the general populace has begun to understand that few who are prone to take their own lives are insane. But, there is a long way to go. Many people still consider suicide to be murder or the act of an insane person and place a stigma on such self-destructive acts. There are even some insurance companies that will deny payment of death benefits if the cause of death is the result of suicide.

Some survivors feel such a great sense of shame that, when talking about the cause of death of their loved one, they either circumvent the truth or avoid it entirely. They avoid friends, other relatives, and acquaintances. Survivors are angry and feel cheated. Cheated because, through death, they have been rejected and denied a chance to help heal the hurt that brought about the death. This is particularly true if the survivor feels that, in some way, they were in the wrong. The victim, through death, has taken away the opportunity to make things right.

King Saul of Israel, fell on his sword and ended his own life rather than be captured and killed by his enemies. Samson, after compromising himself with Delilah, ended his life by using his might and power to bring down the Temple of Dagon. In doing so, he killed more Philistines by his death than he had killed during his lifetime.

Over the years, there have been many men of God who have completed suicide. One, the late Dr. Henry Ness, took his own life rather than bear the pain and agony he was suffering as he lay near death as an aged man. I am convinced beyond a shadow of a doubt that he and many other dedicated Christians who have succumbed to self-destruction are, today, in the presence of God. Through the Holy Spirit, I know with certainty that John is now rejoicing in Heaven with his brothers.

Suicide does not usually happen without warning, but

the warning signs are too often not recognized—a very strong reason why our society needs to better understand suicidal behavior. Only about one third leave a note saying "why."

Some of the warning signs to look for in a suicidal person are: talk of suicide, changes in weight, sleeping problems, lethargy, pre-occupation, chronically pessimistic, favorite things no longer give pleasure, feelings of hopelessness, helplessness, loneliness, and worthlessness.

Although the mental and emotional capacity for suicide is not inherited, the genetic predisposition to certain illnesses, such as depression, can be inherited. Those suffering from major depression, manic depression or schizophrenia are especially susceptible. In fact, a very large percentage of those who take their own lives are plagued with major depression. Just as suicide is a symptom, so also is major depression. Both could very well be the culmination of a long series of difficulties.

Triggering events are often misinterpreted as the reason for the suicide; however, the triggering events are usually the final act following a long series of problems and difficulties in the person's life. The suicidal state of mind is temporary. If the triggering event or circumstance could be avoided, it is conceivable that many suicides could be prevented.

The methods of suicide are as varied as the human mind is capable of inventing. Shooting, hanging, poisoning, overdosing of drugs, slashing wrists, jumping from a building, bridge, cliff or other high place, crashing a vehicle, jumping in front of a car, truck, or train, drowning, and asphyxiation are some of the more common methods employed. But there are other unusual and bizarre methods, such as setting oneself on fire. The resolute mind is capable of concocting the seemingly unthinkable and impossible.

A fifteen year old classmate of our grandson, Eric, took his life just a few months ago. The youth was a member of a household consisting of himself, his parents, an older sister and younger brother. He was a lonely boy, very intelligent and an honor student; but, because he was physically uncoordinated, he was the brunt of many jokes by classmates, especially in physical education classes.

Although not "best friends," he and Eric attended several classes together. Eric was quite impressed with the youth's knowledge and academic skills, but noted he was quiet and tended to be a loner.

Early one morning, around 2:30, after a conversation with his younger brother, he entered the bathroom and carefully covered the floor and other areas. He then undressed, seated himself in the bathtub, poured gasoline over his entire body and then ignited the gasoline. As the flames began to engulf his body, and the pain became unbearable, he cried out in agony. His little brother, awakened by the cries, quickly ran to the bathroom where he was forced to look upon the aftermath of the deadly inferno. The brother that he loved so much lingered for 24 hours before death came to release him from his unbearable pain and suffering.

Soon after his death, a young woman from a prominent Portland, Oregon family was driving to Eugene. Apparently, her resolve to end her life was so great that she stopped at Salem, rented a motel room and, using the exact same method as the boy, took her own life. Was this a "copycat" suicide? It's difficult to say, but it very well could have been.

Here, in McMinnville, a woman selected a most unusual way to end her life. Late at night, wearing dark clothing and with her head down in her folded arms, she seated herself in the center of a curved freeway on-ramp. The driver of the car that hit her was totally unaware of her presence until, just before impact, she raised her head and looked directly toward him.

Gene and June Staples, our former pastors and very close friends, were visiting with us at our home on a hot day in July. Gene and I, in an attempt to seek some coolness, decided to walk down to our waterfall. Our dog, JoJo, joined us, knowing he would receive a great deal of attention. As JoJo played, Gene and I sat on a nearby bench and entered into a lengthy conversation about suicide. I had suggested to him that, in his years of ministry, he must have ministered to many families like ours that were either directly or indirectly involved with suicide. He then shared the following incidents with me:

A lady who owned a home in McMinnville and attended the church where Gene was a pastor, also maintained another residence in Texas. One weekday morning, while in Texas, she was preparing to depart for church when her son began to plead with her not to go. He told her that he was terribly confused and disturbed and asked her to remain home with him instead. She, however, not wanting to fail or disappoint her Bible class, disregarded his pleas and insisted on going.

When she returned home from church, she called out to her son, but received no answer. Apprehensive, she frantically searched the house. When she found him, she was horrified; he had hanged himself in his bedroom closet.

Her faith was shattered; her guilt unbearable. Feeling she had to get away from her Texas home, she returned to McMinnville. At church, even though she would kneel at the altar and pour out her grief, her broken heart seemingly would not mend. Pastor Gene encouraged her to read the Book of Psalms. Three weeks of study restored her faith and allowed her to claim victory over her feelings of guilt.

Another tragic incident occurred while Pastor Gene was serving as a missionary in Uruguay that became a matter of extensive personal conflict for him. The tragedy involved a kind and gentle man, a devout Christian who, because he owned property and employed workers, was considered to be wealthy. In Uruguay, there are only two principal socio-economic classes—the peasants and the wealthy.

One Sunday morning Pastor Gene spoke about the importance of "giving all to Jesus," meaning, of course, that a

Christian must be so devoted to serving Christ that he is willing to give himself in total commitment.

Early the next morning, the police came to Pastor Gene's residence and asked him to accompany them to the gentleman's residence at the edge of town. They walked around the house to the back yard. What he saw there shook him to the very fibre of his soul. The man, after writing a note stating, "Now, I have given all to Jesus," had hanged himself from a tree in his back yard.

Pastor Gene, even as he sought comfort for his own soul, also tried as best he could to reassure the man's family. *Had he been responsible for triggering the suicide of their husband and father?* The family stayed faithful to God, and Pastor Gene stayed faithful to the family. As he prayed with the family, healing came into their hearts and his—they were at peace with God and one another.

Multiple suicides are rare, but do occur. Murder followed by suicide is quite common, but is not truly a multiple suicide. Recently, I read about four teenagers, two couples, who took their lives by asphyxiation. There was no note, nor had there been a word spoken to survivors that would give them a clue of their intentions. They parked in a remote area, ran a hose from the exhaust to the inside of the car, left the engine running, and perished together.

With all the pressures that are placed on our youth, is it any wonder that they are plagued with mental conflict? Being a teenager is more difficult today than at any other time in history. I should know. For 31 years I have taught and counseled young people in public high schools as a teacher and principal. Watching the good fruits of my labor develop, gives me confidence that I could not have selected a more rewarding profession. The incidence of teen suicide is rising at an alarming rate! We need to take notice! *Now!*

Today, more than half of all marriages end in divorce. Only 38 percent of the children in America live with both of their parents. It is frightening to know that 70 percent of all adolescents who attempt suicide come from broken or one-parent homes. It is a fact that American parents spend less time with their children than do parents from most other well-developed nations. This decline in quality parenting and family life, along with a lack of parental supervision, have definitely been contributing factors to the suicide rate. Another major factor is communication—the failure of parents to listen, truly listen, to their children.

A news report recently aired on television about a young man, a senior in high school, who became so severely depressed he felt he had no reason for living and decided to end his life. Placing a handgun against his head, he pulled the trigger sending a bullet through his brain. He normally would have died immediately or, at most, in a matter of minutes; however, he not only survived, he has regained most of his physical functions, including 80 percent of his speech. And, according to his doctors, he has a prognosis of a 100 percent recovery. His doctors said it was a miracle, that it was virtually impossible to live, let alone be normal, with a brain so badly damaged. Yet, he has a strong chance of being completely normal. *Yes, it was a miracle!* God, in His mercy, and for His reasons, intervened to allow this young man to live.

The young man is aware and recognizes that his recovery and being alive is a miracle. He now feels led to devote his Life to Christ and to spread His Word to other young people, encouraging them to appreciate the precious gift, especially when guided by the hand of God.

What can we do in this, the most affluent, most advanced country in all the world, to reduce the number of suicides? Society needs to become better informed regarding suicide. The double standard for physical and mental illness must be eliminated. Attitudes regarding suicide must continue to improve. Instead of avoiding the problem, we must learn to confront and deal with it rationally. Our greatest concern should not be *how* a person dies, but *that* he dies. We must be open-minded, open to discussion and seek out opportunities to learn about suicide. There must not be reluctance on the part of parents, ministers, teachers, or counselors to discuss, teach and inform young people. Suicide prevention centers and hot lines provide a valuable service, but we need more. Most importantly is prayer—prayer will reach the compassionate Christ, and He will intercede to calm the storm that rages in the suicidal mind.

CHAPTER NINE

Our Prayers: Are They Always Answered?

The day was Tuesday, March 19, 1991. The time was 5:47 a.m. United Airlines Flight 611 was flying at an altitude of 36,000 feet with an air speed of 539 miles per hour. The aircraft was a Boeing 747 jumbo jet. The weather at the time of departure from Phoenix had been a mild 58 degrees with clear skies and a slight north-easterly wind. As had been forecast prior to take-off, flight 611 was headed toward a severe storm beginning over eastern New Mexico and extending eastward.

This is your captain," spoke the clear, resonant voice. "We will be experiencing heavy turbulence for some time. Please remain seated with your seat belts fastened."

Lightning flashed, illuminating the sky around the aircraft, while severe turbulence tossed the giant jet around like a child's toy. Violent rain pelted against the windows. Except for apprehensive murmuring, the passengers sat in fearful silence.

"This is your captain speaking. In an effort to get out of this weather, we are in the process of reducing our air speed to 300 miles an hour and descending to an altitude of 5,000 feet. Do not leave your seat for any reason! I repeat, remain buckled in and do not leave your seat. Please pay close attention to any instructions given by the flight attendants."

The pilot's efforts availed nothing. The violence of the storm was equally severe at the lower altitude. The winds continued to rage as sheets of rain pounded the exterior of the aircraft.

"This is your captain, again. We are nearing the Will Rogers World Airport in Oklahoma City where we will land to take refuge from the storm. We should be receiving our landing instructions shortly." Relief was felt throughout the aircraft.

Tom turned to Greg and said, "Thank God! Our prayers have been answered." He was referring to the prayer they had said together asking God to guide them safely through the storm.

Tom Johnson, 36 years of age, lived in an affluent suburb with his wife Ellen and their three young children. They were a Christian family, loved God, and faithfully attended Sunday School and church. Tom, an enterprising electrical engineer, had left home on Wednesday to attend a conference in Scottsdale, Arizona. On Sunday, he went to a church in Phoenix where he met Greg Carmichael and his wife, Janice. Greg, the manager of a large department store in Phoenix had lived in Tempe for more than 20 years. After learning that Tom was alone and in town on business, they invited him to their home for dinner.

During dinner that evening, Tom mentioned that he would be flying home on Tuesday on United Airlines flight 611.

"What time is your flight leaving?" Greg asked with interest.

"Three forty-five a.m. to New York, where I'll catch a connecting flight to Boston. Why?"

"What a coincidence! I'm leaving on that same flight to attend a corporate meeting of department store managers in New York."

"That's great! We'll have to call the airlines and make arrangements for adjoining seats! It'll be great to have your company on my return flight."

At 7:30 a.m. Monday morning, Ellen, gathering her three children around her, prayed for the safe return of their beloved father. Her prayers were supported by unyielding faith and enduring love and devotion. At about the same time his family was praying for him, Tom, with Bible in hand, was kneeling beside the bed in his Phoenix hotel room praying for them and a safe trip home.

Greg and Janice, just before leaving for the airport, prayed together. Their loving worship included praises and a request for an opportunity to make their faith known to others. They ended with a prayer asking God to protect him while he was gone.

Tom and Greg met at Gate 3 and made arrangements for boarding passes that would give them companion seating. Within minutes they had boarded and were airborne. And then the storm . . .

The pilot of flight 611 was making his landing approach when he saw it—a small Cessna, blown off course by the storm, heading directly toward them; the pilot was totally unaware of the impending danger. In an attempt to avoid the smaller plane the pilot pulled back on the stick and tried to climb out of danger, but it was too late—the Cessna struck the left wing of the jumbo jet. What was left of the Cessna plummeted to the ground. Flight 611, out of control, struck the runway and, sliding across a concrete warning apron, crashed into a DC-10 that was awaiting clearance for takeoff.

When Greg awoke hours later, he found himself hospitalized with severe, but not life threatening, injuries. He was heavily bandaged and his movement was restricted. *But*, he thought, *I'm alive! Thank God, I'm alive! But what about Tom? Where is he? Is he okay?* Several hours later the hospital staff notified him that his new found friend had been

112

fatally injured in the crash.

Had their many prayers gone unanswered?

Jerry Maddicks was 35, his wife, Lois, 36. Their family included three children, Timothy 11, Rachel 9, and Alicia 8. The day was Sunday, September 13, 1987—a special day that Alicia had been looking forward to—her birthday. It was late afternoon and pleasantly warm. The Maddicks family was nearing Pomeroy, Washington, on their way to a small town in northern Idaho where Jerry, a minister of the Gospel, was to deliver a sermon that evening. He had been serving God as a pastor and teacher for many years.

Jerry and his family had recently moved to his parents place in Toppenish, Washington from Salinas, California where he had assisted in a church and taught in a Christian school. His father, Wes Maddicks, was the pastor of a church in Toppenish; his mother, Marjean, was the sister of Pastor Donald Foster, the associate pastor of the church where Elsie and I attended.

To gain financial support for a teaching position he had accepted with the Central Indian Bible College in Mobridge, South Dakota, Jerry, since arriving in Toppenish, had been preaching in various churches in the northwest. This eventful night was one of those trips.

That morning, prior to leaving for Idaho, Jerry, at the request of Pastor Don Foster Jr., had ministered to the congregation of a church in Yakima, Washington. Those present at the church, including many personal friends and relatives, were aware of their travel plans and offered special prayers, not only for their safe travel that day, but also that Jerry would have success in his new assignment.

Every member of the family, except Lois, who was driving at the time, was asleep. Suddenly, the van veered to the left and crossed the center line—directly into the path of an oncoming pickup truck. It was never determined why the van veered as it did.

The crash was horrendous! The gasoline tank, located in

the center of the van, exploded on impact. The ensuing fire was so fierce that it completely incinerated the van and all who were in it—the entire Jerry Maddicks family. The driver of the pickup truck also died in the head-on collision. His son, who suffered severe injuries, was the only survivor.

The Washington State Patrol officers investigating the accident had no idea who had died in the van until they discovered Jerry's Bible beside the road where it apparently had been thrown from the van—the only thing to survive the fire. In it, they found where Jerry had written vital statistics about himself, Lois, the children, and other family members. This list greatly aided the officers in their investigation and in notifying the next of kin.

Don Foster Sr. told me later, "Bob, that night, right after the accident, I lay in bed thinking of what I might say if I were asked to hold the funeral service for this precious family. My mind was overwhelmed, my heart broken, as I thought of five caskets lined up across the front of the church and the hearses waiting outside to take them to the cemetery. I prayed for God's help. Thanks to God answering that prayer, when the family did ask me to conduct the service, I was prepared to do so."

Did the many prayers offered for Jerry Maddicks and his family go unanswered? Were the prayers not heard by God?

Angie Hurst, in writing about her missionary parents in her book, *One Witness*, touched upon the question of prayer.

Her father, David Flood, her mother, Svea, their 2 year old son, David Jr., along with Joel and Bertha Erickson, left from Sweden in 1921 as missionaries to the Belgian Congo. The dark continent was a vicious region, aswarm with insects and dangerous animals and, even worse, hostile natives. As they left the outpost of Uvira and headed for the native villages, they were full of zeal and determination to win this vast region for God. The natives, however, not wanting their pagan gods angered by their teachings, refused to accept them. The chiefs were so upset by the missionaries and their message that they threatened to kill them.

Traveling afoot, the group carried their entire belongings on their backs, sleeping in tents, and trading food with the villagers. Their faltering knowledge of the Swahili language made communication with the natives difficult. Despite tirelessly tramping from village to village, they had little to show for their efforts. They were exhausted and sick with malaria, even little David Jr. was ill with the disease. When they arrived at N'dolera, the chief, certain that they would bring evil to the village and anger the gods, told them to move on. The Ericksons wanted to return to their base in Uvira; however, little Svea Flood, just 4' 8" tall, tenaciously clinging to the belief that God had sent them there for a purpose, refused to leave.

They decided to move to the top of the mountain where they felt it would be safer than in the village below. Working together, they built two mud huts to live in and another hut to serve as a church. As they worked, they prayed that the little church would soon be filled. Shortly thereafter, angered and discouraged, the Ericksons returned to Uvira.

Svea began working with the young native boy who delivered chickens and eggs to them. She showered him with love and soon the little fellow knelt beside her and accepted Christ. Svea was determined to win over the villagers one by one and, starting with the boy so that all of Africa would be won for God. When the young boy learned that his friend Svea would soon be giving birth to a child he shared the news with the rest of the village. They had never seen a white baby and were so excited by the news that they sent a midwife to attend to Svea at the appointed time. When the baby came, Svea was ecstatic. She had a new little baby girl. She named her Aina.

Weak and frail from the malaria, Svea lived only seven

days after giving birth to Aina. Grief-stricken, David constructed a coffin, dug a grave, and buried his beloved Svea on the mountain top. Then, filled with anger and bitterness because of his loss, he hired a native carrier to help carry their meager belongs as they set forth for Uvira. In every village they came to, they found a native mother who volunteered to nurse the little baby girl with the blonde hair and big blue eyes.

When they reached Uvira, David, determined to return to Sweden, decided to turn Aina over to the Ericksons to raise as their own child. Unable to conceive children of their own, they were more than delighted to take Aina as their adopted daughter. Unfortunately, a short time later, Bertha Erickson became ill and died—poisoned by an angry village chief. A few days later Joel died, a victim of the same poisoning. Just prior to his death, he asked Arthur and Anna Berg, a missionary couple from America, to take care of and raise little Aina. Anna, like Bertha, had no children and, although she was saddened by the death of her friends, was delighted to receive the baby. The Bergs changed Aina's name to Agatha shortly before returning home to the United states. Soon Agatha became "Aggie."

Later, after she was grown and married, Aggie and her husband, Dr. D.V. Hurst, decided to go to Stockholm, Sweden to visit the father she had never seen. Just prior to their leaving, however, Aggie received a strange publication in the mail. It was printed in Swedish. Inside was an article which, of course, she couldn't read, and a picture of a cross at the head of a grave. On the cross she could make out the name "Svea Flood"—her mother!

Quickly, they found someone who could translate the article for them. It was about two missionaries who, while traveling through the Congo, came upon the graveside and cross on a moutaintop just outside the town of N'dolera. The local villagers told them the story about the missionaries that had lived on the mountaintop so many years ago, the birth of the white baby, and the death of the mother. They also told them about the one little boy that the woman had lead to Christ before her death. They shared how that boy, in later years, obtained permission from the village chief to build a school for the children and how gradually, one by one, all the students were won to Christ and, eventually, their parents as well. Finally, the chief, himself, came to Christ. God is the only one who knows how many souls were ultimately won for His Kingdom through the perseverance of Svea Flood and that one little black boy.

Aggie, at her reunion with her father, found a 73 year old man in very poor health, who had turned his back on God. David Flood was an embittered, angry man, unable to forgive God for the loss of his beloved Svea. However, after Aggie shared with him how their missionary trip to Africa and her mother's death had not been in vain, his attitude changed. After learning how God had used the little African boy, her dad invited Christ back into his heart. Shortly thereafter, he was called by God to join his beloved Svea in their heavenly home.

Was the answer delayed but their prayers answered?

Pastor Gene Staples recently told me about a time when he was called to the home of a young woman to pray for her husband. The couple had a multitude of problems, not the least of which was a business that was failing and about to go under. In addition, the young woman had a prior history of involvement with witchcraft. Although it had been defeated at the time of her conversion and acceptance of Christ, her past experiences with devil worship had now returned to haunt her.

> The day after visiting the young couple in their home, I was called to the McMinnville Community Hospital at 1:00 a.m. The young woman had taken an overdose of her prescription drugs. Her doctor told me that it was unlikely she would sur-

vive, and even if she did, she would have severe brain damage. Taking her cold
hand in mine, and bowing my head, I
lifted my voice to Heaven.

The next 12 hours were crucial. Other
than periodically going to her bedside to see
how she was doing, I spent the entire time
with the family in the waiting room. On one
of the visits I took her hand in mine and,
bending over the bed, quietly whispered in
her ear, "God loves you and so do we." Feeling a weak pressure on my hand, as though
she was attempting to squeeze it, I was certain she had heard me and understood.

Several hours later, a nurse came into
the waiting room, rushed over to where we
were sitting, and excitedly said, "You'll never
believe what's happened! Hurry, come with
me!" Not knowing what had happened, we
quickly jumped to our feet and followed her
back to the young woman's room. We
couldn't believe our eyes! To our amazement, she was wide awake and sitting up in
bed. Seeing us, she immediately started
talking. She was weak from her experience,
but perfectly normal! No brain damage!

*Was this miracle an answer to prayer? Our prayers—
are they always answered?* My answer to both questions is
an emphatic, "Yes!"

"But how," you might ask, "do you *know* that God always answers prayer?"

I know, because first and foremost, the Bible tells me so!
In Matthew 21:22 God says, "And all things, whatsoever ye
shall ask in prayer, believing, ye shall receive." Secondly, by
faith I believe God always answers prayer. My life is built on
faith—if God is for me, who, or what, can be against me?
Matthew 9:20-22 speaks of our being healed by our faith—

118

" . . . a woman who had been sick for 12 years with internal bleeding came up behind Him and touched a tassel of His robe, for she thought, *If I only touch Him, I will be healed.* Jesus turned around and spoke to her, 'Daughter,' he said, 'All is well. You faith has healed you.' And the woman was well from that moment." <u>Third</u>, I have seen, felt, and heard marvelous answers to my prayers which have been revealed in numerous ways. At times, He speaks to me in a still, small voice. Other times, the Holy Spirit stirs my heart with the answer. Occasionally, God must jolt me firmly to make me see. And, when necessary, He sends His angels to be my guide.

The answer to prayer may be immediate, come later, or be answered differently than expected. Sometimes, He may simply say, "No!" But . . . He always answers! I must trust Him, learn to be patient, and wait for His answer, for He alone knows what is best for me. I also must listen carefully and willingly accept whatever His answer may be and not allow that answer to be clouded by my own selfish wishes, desires, and impulses. I may never, in this life, see the results of all my prayers or the results may be made known only years later. If I allow Him to do so, God clearly speaks to me—He speaks to my heart, my soul, my innermost being.

Elsie and I, and our many friends and loved ones, prayed diligently that the lives of our boys would be spared, and yet they were not. Tom Johnson and his family earnestly prayed for his safe return from Boston, but he was killed in the plane crash. The many prayers offered for the Maddicks family were sincere and included boundless faith, yet the entire family lost their lives in the crash of their van.

How can I say that these prayers were answered, when the facts seem to indicate otherwise? Because I do not rely solely on material evidence. Instead, I persevere in faith, believing that whatever happened was for a reason that may be known only to God. He did not take their lives, nor did He preclude their deaths, which He, with His omnipotent power and omnipresence, could so easily have done. *Their lives were not cut short—they were completed.* Even though we miss them, it would be wrong for us to wish them back, for they are now experiencing the happiness and joy of being in the presence of God. Yes, I must exercise faith, be patient, know that God loves me, wants what is best for me, and rely on Him to generate good out of what would seem otherwise. He said He would do it, and I believe it! That's good enough for me!

"And we know that all that happens to us is working for our good if we love God and are fitting into His plans." (Romans 8:28) I am enthralled by His presence, knowing that His vigilance is constant. The Holy Spirit talks with me so that I may know the direction He would have me go, the words He would have me speak, and the action He would have me take. He also provides me with the knowledge that I must have to better serve Him. He loves me and sends His angels to watch over me!

When Pastor Staples prayed for the woman who had overdosed, he prayed with fervor and a strong faith. Her rapid and complete recovery was a demonstration of Christ's healing power. It was a miracle! Thank God, Jesus is alive, and that He is the same today as He was yesterday, and will be tomorrow and forever, never changing.

A young family sat at the table eating the last of their food. Even though the meal was meager, they bowed their heads as the father prayed for God's blessing over the little they had and asked God to provide them with food for their next meal. Before the day ended, a neighbor came to their door with two bags of groceries and told them, "God spoke to me of your need, please accept this food as a gift from my heart."

Some refer to calamities such as earthquakes, hurricanes, tornadoes and floods as "acts of God;" however, these things are not acts of God but rather acts of nature. God has the power to control them and, no doubt, often does so. We, in our limited capacity, may hate these calamities and wonder why God allows them to happen. We forget that God is the ruler of the universe and will govern accordingly. He knows what He's doing even if we don't. And, in His kingdom, there is a reason for everything that happens. For example, we might pray and ask Him for a beautiful day for the benefit of the church picnic and then wonder why He sent rain. Could it be that, in His wisdom and mercy, He sent the rain in answer to a farmer's prayer for his parched crop?

I could continue for hours telling of the wondrous works of the Lord who meets our needs today no differently than He did when He walked with His disciples. An article entitled *Prayer and Baseball* written by Dorothy Morris serves as an excellent illustration of "Let go and Let God" or, to put it another way, "Not my will, but Thy will be done!"

In the article, ten-year-old Darin, a little league pitcher and Christian, had no doubt that prayer could solve problems and change any situation. During a game when he was pitching, his team led by one run and it was the bottom of the last inning. The bases were loaded and there were two outs. A hit would bring in two run and a walk would tie the score. After stepping briefly off the mound, Darin pitched three strikes to win the game. Smiling, his Sunday School teacher assured the boy's mother that she knew he was praying very hard for the win.

Later, at their home, when Darins' mom mentioned what the teacher said. He replied, "I knew the batter was probably praying for a hit and I didn't want to mix God up with two different prayers, so I asked Him to calm me down and help me do my best."

Thanks to Esther McCoy, Dillonvale, Ohio

I pray that God will strengthen me to do the very best I can in all that I do, so that on that day when the Master takes me by the hand and calls me home I will receive the hallmark of Christian service when He looks at me and says, "Well done thou good and faithful servant."

"So now, since we have been made right in God's sight by faith in His promises, we can have real peace with Him because of what Jesus Christ our Lord has done for us." (Romans 5:1)

CHAPTER TEN

Between Here And Eternity

The Bible tells us that, "God has given His angels charge over us, to guard us in our ways." Angels are real! God created these heavenly beings to serve Him and assist man. His angels are always with us. They are there to guide us and accompany us in all that we do and, when needed, provide us with strength, comfort and protection; they help defend us from Satan and his powers.

As spirit beings, angels are usually invisible; however, if necessary, they can manifest themselves by changing their physical appearance to human form. Whenever angels have appeared to man, their appearance has usually been beautiful, brilliant, and dazzling.

Man, while on earth, is subordinate to angels, but, in the kingdom of Heaven, will be superior. Angels are sexless, ageless, do not procreate, never marry and, because they were given eternal life by God, never experience death. When we die, angels will be there to escort us to Heaven. Angels will also call us by name and rejoice with us when we reach God's Throne of Grace. Unlike the Holy Trinity of Father, Son, and Holy Spirit who are omnipresent, angels move back and forth between Heaven and Earth in but a moment of time. One angel or a multitude of angels may come. When God gave the law to Moses, ten thousand angels descended on Mount Sinai to confirm His holy presence.

The apostle Peter was in prison awaiting his execution when an angel appeared to him in his sleep. Iron bars and locked doors do not deter an angel! The angel woke Peter up and told him to prepare to escape. A brilliant light filled the cell as the angel's supernatural powers opened the prison doors and broke the chains that bound Peter.

It was an angel that came to roll the stone away from the entrance to the tomb where Jesus was placed after being crucified. The angel, dressed in white, shone with a dazzling brilliance as bright as a flash of lightning. The Roman guards who were guarding the tomb shook and became as dead men. The stone weighed far more than a single man could move; yet, the angel rolled it away without difficulty. Heavy stones do not deter an angel!

Acts 1:9 gives the account of Jesus' ascension. "And when He had spoken these things, while they beheld, he was taken up; and a cloud received Him out of their sight." The disciples were despondent. Suddenly, two angels, looking like men and dressed in white raiment, appeared to them saying, "Ye men of Galilee, why stand ye gazing up into Heaven? This same Jesus, which is taken up from you into Heaven, shall so come in like manner as ye have seen Him go into Heaven." (Acts 1:11)

Angels have frequently appeared in human form to minister to man. The following are but a few examples of these angelic visitations:

One such incident involved Tina Marshall, a woman from our church, whose lovely voice raised in inspirational song always added so much to the service. A couple of years ago, Tina, after leaving her young son in the care of a sitter, was driving to her work place on a country road south of McMinnville. It was a cold foggy March morning. As she rounded a curve, unaware that the roads were glazed with ice, her car skidded across the center line, left the highway, and crashed into an embankment. Unfortunately, she had forgotten to fasten her seat belt. Dazed and barely conscious, she tried to escape from the mangled wreckage of her car, but couldn't. She was paralyzed and couldn't move! She was in excruciating pain and bleeding profusely. Her car couldn't be seen from the highway. *What was she to do?*

Tina turned to the One source of help that she knew was always available—she prayed to God! Suddenly, a young man appeared behind the car, walked up to the door and said, "Tina, my name is Ray and I'm here to help you. Don't worry, you're going to be all right." After carefully removing her from the car, he gently wrapped her in a wool blanket and carried her to the highway. Amazingly, when he lifted her out of the car, the pain left.

Several drivers stopped. One left to call an ambulance, while the others stayed to help. When Ray turned her over to the care of these people, she was astonished to see that, although she was covered with blood, there wasn't a drop of blood on him or his clothing.

As the paramedics from the ambulance placed her in the ambulance she looked around for Ray, wanting to thank him for saving her. But he was gone! Disappeared! *How,* she thought, *did he find me so soon? My car couldn't be seen from the road and there were no other cars around. Surely on such a cold, damp, foggy day, he wasn't out walking. And, how did he know my name?* She had barely asked, when the answer came: God had sent an angel to rescue her. Praise God in all his mercy, goodness, and love!

A well-known evangelist writes about the Reverend John G. Paton, a missionary to the New Hebrides Islands. In the story, he tells of hostile natives who intended on burning the Patons out and killing them. As they surrounded the mission headquarters that night, John and his wife had prayed that the

125

Lord would protect them from danger. And He did because at daylight, they could see the attackers unaccountably leave. How they Praised God for delivering them!

When the chief of the hostile tribe accepted Jesus as his Savior, Mr. Paton asked him what had stopped the tribe from killing him and his wife and burning down their house a year earlier. The chief said they they had been scared off by the hundreds of large men they had seen in shining garments with drawn swords who had circled the mission station. Mr. Paton knew then that God had indeed protected them by sending angels.

I have heard and read about similar angelic visitations. There is no doubt in my heart or mind that when I die angels will come and carry me to my heavenly home.

Many people have written about what is commonly called near-death experiences. Two who have done extensive research on the subject are Dr. Elizabeth Kubler-Ross, a medical doctor, psychiatrist, and internationally renowned thanatologist, and Dr. Raymond A. Moody, author of *Life after Life*. These two respected authors have interviewed many people who have experienced this phenomena. I believe their research to be a positive confirmation of life after death.

The similarities of experiences as told by dying patients help provide a better understanding of death and the removal of fear. Most persons have indicated that they had a conscious awareness of their environment. There were some who said, while out of their bodies, they could look down and see themselves in the operating room, emergency room, or hospital room being attended by doctors and nurses Many have a floating experience which is usually associated with a great sense of peace and fulfillment. Most also see a brilliant light to which they are drawn—it literally seems to consume them with peace and joy. It seems to be alive and Christians usually refer to it as a Heavenly Being. Nearly all are aware of another being who assists them as they move through a tunnel or valley toward the light. Most were stopped before entering through a gate and were told that it was not their time and that they had to return to the living. Most were reluctant to leave but after returning said they no longer feared death..

A well-known Christian evangelist and religious leader tells how his maternal grandmother sat up in bed at her death and, almost laughingly, said that she saw Jesus with outstretched arms. She also said she saw her husband who had died years later. This same evangelist relates how, as a Bible student, he knew a young missionary volunteer who suddenly became deathly ill. The husband and some faculty members were with her when she suddenly exclaimed that she could see Jesus and hear angels singing.

A missionary to China was praying at the bedside of a dying Chinese Christian man when suddenly the room was filled with heavenly music. The dying man, with a radiant smile on his face, looked up and exclaimed that he could see Jesus standing at the right hand of God, and that his little daughter who had died months before was with Him. Today, because a dying person is given so many drugs, we don't hear as many of these stories. But, to those who face death in Christ, it is a glorious experience.

The Bible guarantees that every believer will be given an escorted journey into the presence of Christ by holy angels. These angelic emissaries are often sent, not only to escort the redeemed of the Lord at death, but to also give hope and joy to sustain those who remain. He has promised to give ". . . the oil of joy for mourning, the garment expressive of praise instead of a heavy, burdened and failing spirit." (Isaiah 61:3)

Evangelist Dwight L. Moody, realizing that his death was near, said, "Earth recedes, Heaven opens before me." Althouse those with him at the time thought that he might be dreaming. he assured them that it was no dream. He said that death was sweet and that there was no valley present. He also said that God was calling him home and he had to go.

127

Moody revived from his death state long enough to share how God had allowed him to see beyond the thin veil separating the seen from the unseen world. He insisted he had gone beyond the portals and within the gates and had glimpsed faces of those whom he had loved and lost. He spoke of what he had proclaimed early on in his ministry—how they would read of his death in the papers but that they should not believe it. He had said he would be more alive then than he was at the present. He would have gone up higher, that is all—"out of this old clay tenement into a house that is immortal; a body that death cannot touch, that sin cannot taint, a body fashioned unto His glorious body . . . "

There are many other astounding personal accounts of what we call the phenomena of near death experience.

Catherine Marshall, the well known author, wrote the following introduction to Betty Malz's book, *My Glimpse of Eternity*:

> It happened when she was twenty-seven years old. In the Union Hospital of Terre Haute, Indiana at 5:00 a.m. on a July morning, 1959. Betty was pronounced dead, a sheet pulled over her head. The Lord had awakened her father, the Rev. Glenn Perkins, at 3:30 that morning and told him to take the forty-minute drive back to the hospital. It was part of God's master plan that Betty's father was to be standing by his daughter's bed to see for himself the drama about to take place.
>
> In *My Glimpse of Eternity*, Betty Malz describes her experiences on the other side of that dividing line that we call "death," then how she returned to her body on the hospital bed . . . to the stunned amazement of her grieving father and the hospital personnel.
>
> "You make dying sound like good news," her husband, John, later told her after listening to her experience.
>
> This book is good news for all of us whose

mortality haunts us.

Upon occasion, God breaks into human life to give us a glimpse of what lies ahead for us. Betty Malz's remarkable experience is a resounding, **"Yes, there is life after death!"** . . . Here is a ringingly triumphant book, a love letter from the Lord of glory to each one of us.

Copyright ©1977, Betty Malz, Fleming H. Revell/Chosen Books—Division of Baker House

How long will God allow the world to continue? Will humanity destroy itself? No! World destruction by humanity is not in God's plan! The signs seem to indicate that the second coming of Christ is near! How wonderful it will be to be caught up in the rapture. But there is so much to do—so many who have not heard about or found Christ! We must pray, live our lives to glorify Him, and continually reach out to others in His name. I pray that our endeavors will be as strong as those of John Harper, a passenger on the Titanic, the ill-fated ship that struck an iceberg and sank in 1912. While the great vessel was sinking, John Harper fought to stay afloat in the frigid water. The currents carried him toward a young man who was desperately holding onto a plank. When Harper came close, he shouted, "Young man, are you saved?" The young man replied, "No." A wave separated them. After a few minutes, they once again drifted close to one another. Harper again called out, "Have you made peace with God?" The young man called back, "Not yet." At that moment a huge wave crashed over John Harper and he was seen no more. However, his words, "Are you saved?" and "Have you made peace with God?" lived on in the young man's mind and heart. Two weeks later, that youth stood up in a Christian Endeavor meeting in New York, told his story, and said, "I am John Harper's last convert."

If only all people could know God and live according to

His Word, we would erase all hunger and strife. But that will not be. The clock of time is running down and time will be no more. The human race is moving rapidly toward a climax and the Bible clearly tells us what that climax will be: **Christ is coming soon!** Who knows, His coming may be tomorrow during the morning hours! Angels will return with Christ to merge time into eternity!

We should give praise to God that His plan for salvation is so simple and easy to attain. As we strive to attain the glories of Heaven, we must be careful to avoid the pitfalls along the way that can lead us to eternal damnation. Even though we have faith in the reality of God and His heavenly hosts, we must never forget that Hell is also a reality—a real place, inhabited by Satan and his demonic hosts.

Living a moral life provides us with strength and stability. These things, these characteristics, are essential to Godly living; however, they, alone, will not gain us eternal life. To attain eternal life, we must believe in God's Son, Jesus, and receive Him into our hearts as our personal Savior. Then, we must communicate with Him through prayer and allow Him to become the Master of our lives.

Next January, my age will reach three quarters of a century plus three. My earthly life is limited, but I am not dismayed; I look forward to a joyous reunion. I have no idea how much longer I may live or where my death may occur, nor would I want to. Those things are known only to God. However, when that time comes, I shall leave this earthly vessel behind. With God's holy angels to guide me, I will ascend through the portals of Heaven and into the presence of Christ, there to be bathed in His love. There I shall once more see the glowing faces of my sons, David, Don and John, and run to join with them in the grand reunion.

"Forgetting these things which are behind, and reaching

130

forward to those things which are ahead,
I press toward the goal of the upward call
of God in Christ Jesus."

(Phillipians 3:13,14)